MOBILE FINANCIAL SERVICES

CONSUMER USE OF MOBILE PAYMENTS AND BANKING

FINANCIAL INSTITUTIONS AND SERVICES

Additional books in this series can be found on Nova's website under the Series tab.

Additional E-books in this series can be found on Nova's website under the E-book tab.

FINANCIAL INSTITUTIONS AND SERVICES

MOBILE FINANCIAL SERVICES

CONSUMER USE OF MOBILE PAYMENTS AND BANKING

SILAS PAULSEN
EDITOR

publishers

New York

Copyright © 2013 by Nova Science Publishers, Inc.

For permission to use material from this book please contact us:
Telephone 631-231-7269; Fax 631-231-8175
Web Site: http://www.novapublishers.com

NOTICE TO THE READER

The Publisher has taken reasonable care in the preparation of this book, but makes no expressed or implied warranty of any kind and assumes no responsibility for any errors or omissions. No liability is assumed for incidental or consequential damages in connection with or arising out of information contained in this book. The Publisher shall not be liable for any special, consequential, or exemplary damages resulting, in whole or in part, from the readers' use of, or reliance upon, this material. Any parts of this book based on government reports are so indicated and copyright is claimed for those parts to the extent applicable to compilations of such works.

Independent verification should be sought for any data, advice or recommendations contained in this book. In addition, no responsibility is assumed by the publisher for any injury and/or damage to persons or property arising from any methods, products, instructions, ideas or otherwise contained in this publication.

This publication is designed to provide accurate and authoritative information with regard to the subject matter covered herein. It is sold with the clear understanding that the Publisher is not engaged in rendering legal or any other professional services. If legal or any other expert assistance is required, the services of a competent person should be sought. FROM A DECLARATION OF PARTICIPANTS JOINTLY ADOPTED BY A COMMITTEE OF THE AMERICAN BAR ASSOCIATION AND A COMMITTEE OF PUBLISHERS.

Additional color graphics may be available in the e-book version of this book.

Library of Congress Cataloging-in-Publication Data

ISBN: 978-1-62618-703-0

Published by Nova Science Publishers, Inc. † New York

CONTENTS

PREFACE

Mobile phones have clearly become ubiquitous and a standard aspect of daily life for many American consumers in the last decade. Ongoing innovations in mobile finance show some potential to change the way consumers conduct financial transactions by offering consumers new services. Yet, many people remain skeptical of the benefit of mobile financial services and the level of security provided along with such services. This book examines the use of mobile technology to access financial services and make financial decisions, with a focus on how consumers are interacting with financial institutions; current use of mobile banking and payments; and other mobile financial services and new technologies.

Chapter 1 – Statement of Sandra F. Braunstein, Director, Division of Consumer and Community Affairs, Board of Govenors of the Federal Reserve System.

Chapter 2 – Mobile devices have increasingly become tools that consumers use for banking, payments, budgeting, and shopping. This report presents findings from an online survey, conducted in December 2011 and January 2012, examining the use of mobile technology to access financial services and make financial decisions.

Key findings of the survey include

- Mobile phones and mobile Internet access are in widespread use
  - 87 percent of the U.S. population has a mobile phone
  - 44 percent of mobile phones are smartphones (Internet-enabled)
  - 84 percent of smartphone users have accessed the Internet on their phone in the past week
- The ubiquity of mobile phones is changing the way consumers access financial services

- 21 percent of mobile phone owners have used mobile banking in the past 12 months
- 11 percent of those not currently using mobile banking think that they will probably use it within the next 12 months
- The most common use of mobile banking is to check account balances or recent transactions (90 percent of mobile banking users)
- Transferring money between accounts is the second most common use of mobile banking (42 percent of mobile banking users)
- Mobile phones are also changing the way consumers make payments
  - 12 percent of mobile phone owners have made a mobile payment in the past 12 months
  - The most common use of mobile payments was to make an online bill payment (47 percent of mobile payment users)
  - 21 percent of mobile payment users transferred money directly to another person's bank, credit card, or Paypal account
- Perceptions of limited usefulness and concerns about security are holding back the adoption of mobile financial services
  - The primary reason why mobile phone users had not yet adopted mobile banking was that they felt their banking needs were being met without the use of mobile banking (58 percent)
  - Concerns about the security of the technology were the primary reason given for not using mobile payments (42 percent) and the second most common reason given for not using mobile banking (48 percent)
  - More than a third of mobile phone users who do not use mobile payments either don't see any benefit from using mobile payments or find it easier to pay with another method
- The "underbanked" make significant use of mobile financial services
  - The underbanked make comparatively heavy use of both mobile banking and mobile payments, with 29 percent having used mobile banking and 17 percent having used mobile payments in the past 12 months
  - 62 percent of the underbanked who use mobile payments have used it to pay bills
  - 10 percent of the completely unbanked report using mobile banking in the past 12 months, and 12 percent have made a mobile payment

Chapter 3 – Statement of Kenneth C. Montgomery, First Vice President and Chief Operating Officer, Federal Reserve Bank of Boston.

Chapter 4 – Statement of Michael L. Katz, Sarin Chair in Strategy and Leadership, University of California, Berkeley.

Chapter 5 – Statement of Thomas P. Brown, Adjunct Professor, Berkeley Law School, University of California.

Chapter 6 – Statement of Sarah Jane Hughes, Maurer School of Law, Indiana University.

Chapter 7 – Testimony of Troy Leach, Chief Technology Officer, PCI Security Standards Council.

Chapter 8 – Testimony of Ed McLaughlin, Chief Emerging Payments Officer, Mastercard Worldwide.

Chapter 9 – Testimony of Randy Vanderhoof, Executive Director, Smart Card Alliance.

Chapter 10 – Testimony of Suzanne Martindale, Staff Attorney, Consumers Union.

In: Mobile Financial Services
Editor: Silas Paulsen

ISBN: 978-1-62618-703-0
© 2013 Nova Science Publishers, Inc.

Chapter 1

STATEMENT OF SANDRA F. BRAUNSTEIN, DIRECTOR, DIVISION OF CONSUMER AND COMMUNITY AFFAIRS, BOARD OF GOVENORS OF THE FEDERAL RESERVE SYSTEM. HEARING ON "DEVELOPING THE FRAMEWORK FOR SAFE AND EFFICIENT MOBILE PAYMENTS"[*]

Chairman Johnson, Ranking Member Shelby, and members of the Committee, thank you for inviting me to appear before you today to talk about consumers' use of mobile financial services.

The evolution of new technologies that enable consumers to conduct financial transactions using mobile devices has the potential to affect their financial lives in important--but as of yet, not fully known--ways. For this reason, the Federal Reserve has been monitoring trends and developments in mobile financial services. By "mobile financial services," I am really talking about two categories of activities. The first we call "mobile banking," which is using your mobile device to interact with your financial institution, mostly doing things you could also do through more traditional means, like check your account balance or transfer money between accounts. The second we call "mobile payments," which we define as making purchases, bill payments,

---

[*] This is an edited, reformatted and augmented version of a statement presented March 29, 2012 before the Senate Committee on Banking, Housing, and Urban Affairs.

charitable donations, or payments to other persons using your mobile device with the payment applied to your phone bill, charged to your credit card, or withdrawn directly from your bank account.

Beyond banking and payments, mobile devices have the potential to be useful tools in helping consumers track their spending, saving, investing, and borrowing, and in making financial decisions. Such technologies also hold the potential to expand access to mainstream financial services to segments of the population that are currently unbanked or underbanked. That said, the technologies are still new, and important concerns, such as consumers' expressions of unease about the security of these technologies, must also be addressed for consumers to feel confident adopting these new services.

To further our understanding of consumers' use of, and opinions about, such services, the Federal Reserve commissioned a survey late last year. Nearly 2,300 respondents completed the survey. This survey is among the first to integrate questions about using mobile devices for shopping and comparing products along with questions about using mobile devices for banking and payments. On March 14, 2012, the Federal Reserve released a report, based on these responses, titled "Consumers and Mobile Financial Services." My testimony today will draw from this report, which is attached to my written testimony.

Nearly nine out of ten adults in the United States have a mobile phone, and two-fifths of those phones are so-called "smartphones" with Internet connectivity. Among all mobile phone users, one out of five has used their phones to conduct some banking activity in the last 12 months. Those users with more traditional mobile phones, or so-called "feature phones," access bank information via text messages, while smartphone users access their bank information by downloading their bank's application or via the bank's Internet site. Younger consumers, those below age 29, have readily adopted mobile banking, and make up almost 44 percent of all consumers surveyed who use such services. Adoption rates of mobile banking also differ by racial and ethnic background, with Hispanics and non-Hispanic blacks making up a disproportionate share of those who use mobile banking services. The most common transactions performed by users of mobile banking were checking account balances or checking recent transactions. Transferring money between accounts was another common transaction.

Of those consumers who had not adopted mobile banking, the primary reason given was that they felt their banking needs were being met through more traditional means. Security concerns were the second most-cited reason for not using mobile banking. Specifically, consumers expressed concerns about hackers gaining access to their phones and exposing their personal financial information. A little more than one-third of all mobile phone users reported that they do not know how secure mobile banking technology is for protecting their personal information, while an additional one-third rated the technology as unsafe. Nevertheless, among those consumers with any type of mobile phone, but who are not currently using mobile banking, one out of ten expects to be using it within the next year.

In addition to mobile banking, we asked about mobile payments, which I described earlier. Mobile payments are not yet as prevalent as mobile banking; one out of eight respondents reported making a mobile payment in the previous 12 months, and usually this involved paying a bill online via their mobile phone. Mobile payments are disproportionately used by consumers under age 45 and by Hispanics. Consumers who are not currently using mobile payments responded that they were concerned about the security of the technology, did not see any benefit from mobile payments, or found it easier to pay in other ways—for example, with cash or with a credit card.

Consumers who are "underbanked"--that is, those who have a bank account but who also use an alternative financial service provider such as a check casher, payday lender, auto-title lender, or payroll card--make significant use of mobile banking and mobile payments. Among this group, nearly three out of ten have used mobile banking, primarily to check their account balances. The underbanked are more likely than the general population to use mobile payments, with one out of six using payment services on their mobile devices. Those consumers who are unbanked also report using mobile financial services, generally in conjunction with a general purpose prepaid card or payroll card.

Let me give you a few examples from the report of how consumers reported using mobile financial services to make financial decisions. I stated earlier that the most frequent use of mobile banking was to check account balances. Of those consumers who use mobile banking, more than two-thirds reported that they checked their account balance or available credit before making a large purchase. Moreover, among the consumers that reported doing this, nearly six out of ten reported that they had decided not to buy an item because of the amount of money available in their account. As another example, some consumers reported setting up a text alert from their bank if their account balance was getting low; among those using this service, five out of six reported taking some action--transferring money into the account with the low balance, reducing spending, or making a deposit into the account--in response to receiving an alert. Consumers also reported using their mobile devices to browse product reviews or get pricing information while shopping.

More details on consumers' use of mobile financial services are available in the report. Staff members in the Division of Consumer and Community Affairs expect to conduct additional analysis of the data in the months ahead. This should round out our understanding of these initial findings. For instance, some of the differences that we see based on ethnic or socioeconomic factors may be better understood when we examine how such factors interact with other characteristics of the respondents. We also anticipate that we may conduct periodic updates of the survey to monitor consumers' experiences as the technology and business practices evolve.

Thank you again for inviting me to appear before you today. I would be happy to answer any questions you may have.

In: Mobile Financial Services
Editor: Silas Paulsen

ISBN: 978-1-62618-703-0
© 2013 Nova Science Publishers, Inc.

Chapter 2

CONSUMERS AND MOBILE FINANCIAL SERVICES*

Matthew B. Gross, Jeanne M. Hogarth and Maximilian D. Schmeiser

EXECUTIVE SUMMARY

Mobile devices have increasingly become tools that consumers use for banking, payments, budgeting, and shopping. This report presents findings from an online survey, conducted in December 2011 and January 2012, examining the use of mobile technology to access financial services and make financial decisions.

Key findings of the survey include

- Mobile phones and mobile Internet access are in widespread use
  - 87 percent of the U.S. population has a mobile phone
  - 44 percent of mobile phones are smartphones (Internet-enabled)
  - 84 percent of smartphone users have accessed the Internet on their phone in the past week
- The ubiquity of mobile phones is changing the way consumers access financial services

---

* This is an edited, reformatted and augmented version of the Board of Govenors of the Federal Reseve System, dated March 2012.

- 21 percent of mobile phone owners have used mobile banking in the past 12 months
- 11 percent of those not currently using mobile banking think that they will probably use it within the next 12 months
- The most common use of mobile banking is to check account balances or recent transactions (90 percent of mobile banking users)
- Transferring money between accounts is the second most common use of mobile banking (42 percent of mobile banking users)
- Mobile phones are also changing the way consumers make payments
  - 12 percent of mobile phone owners have made a mobile payment in the past 12 months
  - The most common use of mobile payments was to make an online bill payment (47 percent of mobile payment users)
  - 21 percent of mobile payment users transferred money directly to another person's bank, credit card, or Paypal account
- Perceptions of limited usefulness and concerns about security are holding back the adoption of mobile financial services
  - The primary reason why mobile phone users had not yet adopted mobile banking was that they felt their banking needs were being met without the use of mobile banking (58 percent)
  - Concerns about the security of the technology were the primary reason given for not using mobile payments (42 percent) and the second most common reason given for not using mobile banking (48 percent)
  - More than a third of mobile phone users who do not use mobile payments either don't see any benefit from using mobile payments or find it easier to pay with another method
- The "underbanked" make significant use of mobile financial services
  - The underbanked make comparatively heavy use of both mobile banking and mobile payments, with 29 percent having used mobile banking and 17 percent having used mobile payments in the past 12 months
  - 62 percent of the underbanked who use mobile payments have used it to pay bills
  - 10 percent of the completely unbanked report using mobile banking in the past 12 months, and 12 percent have made a mobile payment

INTRODUCTION

Mobile phones have clearly become ubiquitous and a standard aspect of daily life for many American consumers in the last decade. Ongoing innovations in mobile finance show some potential to change the way consumers conduct financial transactions by offering consumers new services. Yet, many people remain skeptical of the benefit of mobile financial services and the level of security provided along with such services.

To further understanding of these developments and consumers' usage of and attitudes towards mobile financial services, the Board conducted a consumer survey in late 2011 and early 2012.

Trends in the Utilization of Mobile Banking and Payments

A number of new services allow consumers to obtain financial account information and conduct transactions with their financial institution ("mobile banking") and others allow consumers to make payments, transfer money, or pay for goods and services ("mobile payments").

As the market share of Internet-enabled smartphones continues to grow, the utilization of mobile banking and mobile payment technologies also increases.[1] As of March 2011, nearly one out of every five Americans with both a bank account and a mobile phone has used their phone to view account balances, receive account alerts, and conduct banking with their financial institution in the past 90 days.[2]

Although mobile payments have been adopted more slowly by consumers in the U.S. than in many other countries, these services may become more popular over the coming years as the technology evolves and if the services become more widely accepted as a form of payment. In September 2011, for example, Google launched the Google Wallet service, which allows consumers to use smartphones equipped with a near field communication (NFC) chip to make "tap payments" at any retailer accepting MasterCard Pay-Pass. Besides Google, many other firms—including mobile phone carriers, credit card issuers, and payment networks—are investing in mobile wallet technology. As the number of phones equipped with NFC increases, mobile payments may also increase.

Consumers respond to timely financial incentives and emotional appeals. Recent survey data show that some consumers view mobile payments as time-saving and convenient while providing them with increased access to, and control of, their finances. Despite these positive mobile finance attributes and perceptions, consumers also remain concerned about the cost and the security risks inherent in mobile financial transactions.[3]

Potential Utilization for "Underbanked" and "Unbanked" Consumers

Mobile phone use is high among younger generations, minorities, and those with low levels of income—groups that are prone to be unbanked or underbanked. Mobile banking and mobile payments have the potential to expand financial access to the unbanked and underbanked by reducing transaction costs and increasing the accessibility of financial products and services.

A significant number of Americans do not have a bank account of any kind, and many make regular use of alternative financial services such as payday loans, check cashers, rent-to-own services, money orders, or pawn shops. A 2009 study by the Federal Deposit Insurance Corporation (FDIC) found that 8 percent of Americans had no checking or savings account, and thus were defined as unbanked.[4] An additional 18 percent had a bank account but had used an alternative financial service at least once per year and so were classified as underbanked.

While there remains a digital divide in computer Internet access across the socioeconomic spectrum, this divide does not hold true for mobile phone access. The 2011 Pew Internet study showed that 83 percent of American adults have a mobile phone, and 35 percent have a smartphone that can access the Internet. Moreover, adoption of mobile phones is actually higher among minorities, as 89 percent of non-Hispanic blacks and 86 percent of Hispanics own a mobile phone.

Indeed, minorities are also more likely to own a smartphone than non-Hispanic whites, with 44 percent of both non-Hispanic blacks and Hispanics owning a smartphone compared with 30 percent of non-Hispanic whites. While mobile phone and smart-phone adoption is less prevalent at lower levels of income, approximately 75 percent of U.S. adults in households earning less than $20,000 per year have a mobile phone of some type, and 20 percent have a smartphone.[5]

Younger Age Groups: Mobile Phone and Mobile Banking Adoption

Unsurprisingly, mobile phone adoption is highest for younger age groups: only 5 percent of individuals ages 18 to 24 do not have a mobile phone, and 49 percent have a smartphone.

In contrast, 44 percent of those ages 65 and over do not have a mobile phone, and only 11 percent have a smartphone.[6]

Furthermore, and perhaps more surprisingly, a recent survey by the Center for Financial Services Innovation (CFSI) shows that individuals under the age of 25 are increasingly underbanked—some as a matter of choice—and appear comfortable with alternative financial services.[7]

Given the prevalence of mobile phone usage among young individuals, minorities, and low-income families—groups most likely to be unbanked or underbanked—there is potential for mobile financial services to help integrate these individuals into the financial mainstream.

Survey Background

In consultation with a mobile financial services advisory group made up of key Federal Reserve System staff with relevant consumer research backgrounds, the Consumer Research Section in the Federal Reserve Board's Division of Consumer and Community Affairs designed a survey instrument to examine consumers' usage of and attitudes towards mobile phones and mobile financial services.

The survey was administered by Knowledge Networks, an online consumer research company, on behalf of the Board. The survey was conducted using a sample of adults ages 18 and over from KnowledgePanel®, a proprietary, probability-based web panel of more than 50,000 individuals from randomly sampled households; the sample was designed to be representative of the U.S. population.

After pretesting, the data collection for the survey began on December 22, 2011 and concluded on January 9, 2012. The 2,290 respondents completed the survey in approximately 15 minutes (median time).

The number of respondents sampled and participating in the survey, and the survey completion rates, are presented in table 1.

A total of 3,382 e-mail solicitations to participate in the survey were sent out to the KnowledgePanel, and 2,290 individuals completed the survey fully (a "cooperation rate" yield of 68 percent). To enhance the cooperation rate, Knowledge Networks sent e-mail reminders to non-responders on days three and six of the field period.

The responses to all the survey questions are presented in Appendix 2 in the order in which they were asked of respondents.

A table of summary statistics for the respondent demographics is also included as table B.87.

Beginning at table B.88, cross-tabulations are presented of consumers' use of online banking, telephone banking, mobile banking, and mobile payments by age, race, gender, education, and income.

The following sections of this report summarize key findings from the Knowledge Networks survey of consumers, with a focus on how consumers are using mobile phones to conduct their banking, make payments, enhance information gathering while shopping, and manage their finances. All data were weighted to yield estimates for the U.S. population.

Only questions pertaining to these topics are discussed in the report; however, the complete survey questionnaire and the results of the entire survey are summarized in Appendix 1 and Appendix 2.

HOW ARE CONSUMERS INTERACTING WITH FINANCIAL INSTITUTIONS?

Survey respondents were asked a set of screening questions that covered whether or not they had a bank account, access to the Internet, and ownership of mobile phones or smartphones. Survey responses indicate that the majority of American consumers use some form of technology to interact with their financial institution.

Table 1. Key survey response statistics: Main interview

Number sampled for main survey	Qualified completes	Cooperation rate
3,382	2,290	68%

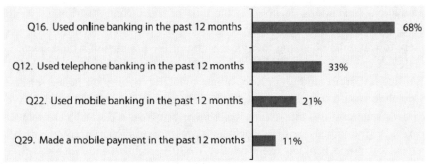

Note: The denominator varies across services due to question screening.

Figure 1. Usage of different means of accessing banking services.

As shown in figure 1, of those consumers with regular Internet access and a bank account, 68 percent used online banking in the past 12 months. Telephone banking is the second most commonly used method of accessing financial services, with 33 percent of banked consumers reporting that they used it in the past 12 months. Mobile banking and mobile payments are the least common methods of accessing financial services, as just over a fifth of respondents with mobile phones and a bank account report using mobile banking and only 11 percent report using mobile payments in the past 12 months.

However, as discussed in the following section, mobile banking access appears to be gaining traction with consumers and is likely to overtake telephone banking access in the next couple of years (as measured by consumers' expectations regarding their future use of the technology).

Online Banking

Three out of ten respondents (30 percent) who use online banking are between ages 30 and 44, while 20 percent of the online banking users are age 60 and older (see tables B.88, B.91, B.94, B.97, and B.100 in Appendix 2). Online banking users are predominantly non-Hispanic whites (73 percent), while Hispanics and non-Hispanic blacks comprise about 12 percent and 8 percent of the online banking community, respectively.

Online banking users are split evenly among men and women. Use of online banking is generally unrelated to household income, with the share of online banking users by income category corresponding to their share of the population. Exceptions occurred at the tails of the income distribution, with those individuals earning less than $25,000 per year being significantly less likely to use online banking than their share of the population would suggest, while those individuals earning more than $100,000 per year being significantly more likely to use online banking than their share of the population would suggest. Level of education and use of online banking have a linear relationship, with online banking use increasing as education level increases: individuals with a bachelor's degree or higher account for 39 percent of online banking users relative to 30 percent of individuals with a bank account.

CURRENT USE OF MOBILE BANKING AND PAYMENTS

Mobile Banking

The Federal Reserve survey defines mobile banking as "using a mobile phone to access your bank account, credit card account, or other financial account. Mobile banking can be done either by accessing your bank's web page through the web browser on your mobile phone, via text messaging, or by using an application downloaded to your mobile phone."

A significant number of mobile phone users have already adopted mobile banking. Nearly 21 percent of mobile phone users in the survey report that they used mobile banking in the past 12 months.[8] Moreover, among those consumers who do not currently use mobile banking, 11 percent report that they will "definitely" or "probably" use mobile banking in the next 12 months. An additional 17 percent of those who report that they are unlikely to use mobile banking in the next 12 months report that they will "definitely" or "probably" adopt mobile banking at some point. Adding all these respondents together would imply peak adoption of 42 percent of all mobile phone owners.[9] As smartphone users are more likely to adopt mobile banking than non-smartphone users, increasing smartphone adoption should further fuel mobile banking adoption.

Use of mobile banking appears to be highly correlated with age (table 2), as individuals between ages 18 and 29 account for approximately 44 percent of mobile banking users, relative to 22 percent of mobile phone users. Conversely, individuals age 60 and over account for only 6 percent of all mobile banking users, while at the same time they represent 24 percent of all mobile phone users.

Non-Hispanic black and Hispanic users show a dis-proportionately high rate of adoption of mobile banking (table 3), at 16 percent and 17 percent of all mobile banking users relative to 11 percent and 13 percent of mobile phone users, respectively. Mean-while, mobile banking users are split evenly between males and females, and use of mobile banking is generally unrelated to household income (table 4), with the share of mobile banking users by income category corresponding to their share of the mobile phone user population. As with online banking, exceptions occurred at the tails of the income distribution, with those individuals earning less than $25,000 per year being significantly less likely to use mobile banking than their share of the mobile phone user population would suggest, while those individuals earning more than $100,000 per year being significantly more likely to use mobile banking than their share of the mobile phone user population would suggest. Mobile banking is highly correlated with education (table 5): 73 percent of all mobile banking users have at least some college education, but this education group represents only 60 percent of all mobile phone users.

By far, checking financial account balances or transaction inquiries were the most common mobile banking activity, with 90 percent of mobile banking users having performed this function in the past 12 months (figure 2). Less prevalent activities were transferring money between accounts (42 percent) or receiving a text message alert from a bank (33 percent). Less frequently used mobile banking functions include making online bill payments from a bank account (26 percent), locating an in-network ATM (21 percent), and depositing a check by phone (11 percent). Lastly, mobile investment management is utilized by only 2 percent of mobile banking users. Many mobile banking users appear to be making use of their banks' mobile applications, as 48 percent have installed such an application on their phones.

Table 2. Use of mobile banking in the past 12 months by age

Percent, except as noted			
Age categories	**Yes**	**No**	**Total**
18–29	43.5	16.8	22.4
30–44	35.7	24.7	27
45–59	14.7	30.2	26.9
60+	6.1	28.4	23.7
Number of respondents	**372**	**1,626**	**1,998**

Note: This is table B.89 in Appendix 2.

Table 3. Use of mobile banking in the past 12 months by race

Percent, except as noted			
Race/ethnicity	**Yes**	**No**	**Total**
White, Non-Hispanic	60.3	71.5	69.2
Black, Non-Hispanic	16.2	10	11.3
Other, Non-Hispanic	5.2	5.8	5.6
Hispanic	17.1	11.6	12.8
2+ Races, Non-Hispanic	1.2	1.1	1.2
Number of respondents	**372**	**1,626**	**1,998**

Note: This is table B.92 in Appendix 2.

Table 4. Use of mobile banking in the past 12 months by income group

Percent, except as noted			
Income group	**Yes**	**No**	**Total**
Less than $25,000	12.8	19.9	18.4
$25,000–$39,999	19	16.6	17.1
$40,000–$74,999	27.5	26.5	26.7
$75,000–$99,999	12.9	14	13.8
$100,000 or greater	27.9	22.9	24
Number of respondents	**372**	**1,626**	**1,998**

Note: Table B.101 in Appendix 2.

Table 5. Use of mobile banking in the past 12 months by education group

Percent, except as noted			
Education (categorical)	**Yes**	**No**	**Total**
Less than high school	5.5	12.1	10.7
High school	21.5	31.8	29.6
Some college	39	27.4	29.8
Bachelor's degree or higher	34	28.8	29.9
Number of respondents	372	1,626	1,998

Note: Table B.98 in Appendix 2.

Consumers report using mobile banking up to 60 times per month; however, the median number of mobile banking transactions is four or five times in a typical month.

Of the consumers who use mobile banking, many appear to be quite satisfied with their experiences, as 62 percent report being "very satisfied" with their experiences, and another 32 percent report being "somewhat satisfied" with their experiences.

Among those consumers with mobile phones who do not currently use mobile banking, the top two reasons for not using the service are that they believe their banking needs are met without mobile banking (58 percent) and that they are concerned about security (48 percent) (figure 3). Less commonly cited reasons include a lack of trust in the technology to process transactions properly (22 percent), the high cost of data access on mobile phones (18 percent), and the small size of the mobile phone screen (17 percent).

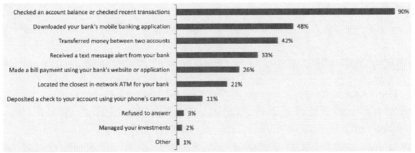

Note: This was question 25 in the survey (see Appendix 1); number of respondents was 372.

Figure 2. Using your mobile phone, have you done any of the following in the past 12 months?

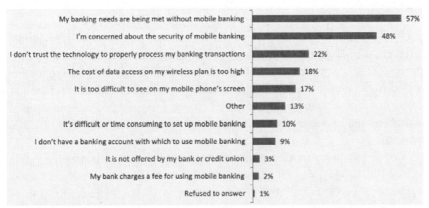

Note: This was question 36 in the survey (see Appendix 1); number of respondents was 1,626.

Figure 3. What are the main reasons you have decided not to use mobile banking?

Consumers who express concerns about the security of mobile banking are concerned with hackers gaining access to their phone remotely (54 percent), losing their phone or having it stolen (19 percent), and experiencing data interception by a third party (18 percent). If these concerns were addressed, many non-users would be willing to adopt mobile banking.

Moreover, the potential uses of mobile banking by those who have yet to adopt it largely mirror those of current users. The majority is interested in checking financial account balances or recent transactions (55 percent), while fewer are interested in receiving text message alerts from their bank (30 percent), transferring money between accounts (25 percent), or making bill payments (24 percent).

Mobile Payments

The Federal Reserve survey defined mobile payments as "purchases, bill payments, charitable donations, payments to another person, or any other payments made using a mobile phone. Mobile payments can be used by accessing a web page through the web browser on your mobile device, by sending a text message (SMS), or by using a downloadable application on your mobile device. The amount of the payment may be applied to your phone bill (for example, Red Cross text message donation), charged to your credit card, or withdrawn directly from your bank account."

Consumers were less likely to adopt mobile payments than mobile banking, with only 12 percent of mobile phone users reporting that they made a mobile payment in the past 12 months. Mobile payment users also perform a narrower set of transactions than mobile banking users, with the most common activity being payment of bills (47 percent), followed by making online purchases (36 percent) and transferring money directly to another person (21 percent). All other transactions (e.g., receiving a payment, texting to make a charitable donation) are used by less than 10 percent of those making mobile payments.

Mobile payments are disproportionately used by younger consumers (table 6). Individuals age 18 to 29 account for 37 percent of mobile payment users relative to 22 percent of all mobile phone users, while individuals age 30 to 44 account for a further 36 percent of mobile payment users relative to 27 percent of all mobile phone users. Hispanic consumers are active users of mobile payments, accounting for approximately 21 percent of all mobile payment users relative to 13 percent of all mobile phone users (table 7). In contrast, non-Hispanic whites are proportionally less likely to use mobile payments, as they make up 58 percent of mobile payment users but are 69 percent of mobile phone users. Almost 13 percent of non-Hispanic blacks use mobile payments, which is comparable to their 11 percent share of the mobile phone user population. Females are slightly more likely to use mobile payments than males, accounting for 55 percent of all users (table 8). Income does not play a role in mobile payment use, as each income group represents roughly the same percentage as it does in the overall mobile phone user sample (table 9). Similarly, mobile payment use by education level is roughly proportionate to its representation in the mobile phone user population (table 10).

Consumers use a variety of methods to make mobile payments, but the most common method is to input a credit card, debit card, or prepaid card number into a mobile phone (66 percent). Other mobile payment techniques used by consumers include making payments directly from a bank account (45 percent); using Google Wallet, Paypal, or iTunes (22 percent); or adding a payment to a mobile phone bill (8 percent).

Table 6. Use of mobile payments in the past 12 months by age

Percent, except as noted			
Age categories	Yes	No	Total
18–29	37.3	20.3	22.4
30–44	35.9	25.6	26.9
45–59	16.9	28.5	27
60+	10	25.7	23.7
Number of respondents	**213**	**1,780**	**1,993**

Note: This is table B.90 in Appendix 2.

Table 7. Use of mobile payments in the past 12 months by race

Percent, except as noted			
Race/ethnicity	Yes	No	Total
White, Non-Hispanic	58.3	70.8	69.3
Black, Non-Hispanic	12.9	10.9	11.2
Other, Non-Hispanic	7.1	5.4	5.6
Hispanic	20.9	11.6	12.8
2+ Races, Non-Hispanic	0.9	1.2	1.2
Number of respondents	**213**	**1,780**	**1,993**

Note: This is table B.93 in Appendix 2.

Table 8. Use of mobile payments in the past 12 months by gender

Percent, except as noted			
Sex	**Yes**	**No**	**Total**
Female	55	52.7	53
Male	45	47.3	47
Number of respondents	**213**	**1,780**	**1,993**

Note: This is table B.96 in Appendix 2.

Table 9. Use of mobile payments in the past 12 months by income group

Percent, except as noted			
Income group	**Yes**	**No**	**Total**
Less than $25,000	19.1	18.5	18.5
$25,000–$39,999	20.6	16.7	17.2
$40,000–$74,999	23	27.2	26.7
$75,000–$99,999	11.7	14	13.7
$100,000 or greater	25.6	23.6	23.9
Number of respondents	**213**	**1,780**	**1,993**

Note: This is table B.102 in Appendix 2.

**Table 10. Use of mobile payments in the past 12 months
by education group**

Percent, except as noted			
Education (categorical)	**Yes**	**No**	**Total**
Less than high school	7.2	11.2	10.7
High school	27.9	29.9	29.7
Some college	37	28.7	29.7
Bachelor's degree or higher	27.9	30.1	29.9
Number of respondents	213	1,780	1,993

Note: This is table B.99 in Appendix 2.

Consumers use mobile payment services less frequently than they do mobile banking services. The median number of mobile payments in a typical month is one. Although some respondents reported making as many as 24 mobile payments per month, fewer than 7 percent of respondents make more than five payments in a typical month.

As with mobile banking, users of mobile payments appear to be quite satisfied with their experiences: 55 percent report being "very satisfied" with their experiences and 33 percent report being "somewhat satisfied" with their experiences.

Although security is the dominant reason why individuals do not use mobile payments (42 percent), there are many consumers who do not see any value in mobile payments; 36 percent report that it is easier to pay with other methods, and 37 percent report that they do not see any benefit from using mobile payments (figure 4). Other reasons for not using include the lack of necessary features on a phone (31 percent) and a lack of trust in the technology to properly process payments (20 percent).

If the concerns of non-users of mobile payments were addressed, those consumers express that they would have an interest in using mobile payments for a variety of activities. In particular, 34 percent report that they would pay bills online using their phone, 28 percent would receive coupons on their phone, and 22 percent say they would receive location-based offers or buy goods and services online. Making person-to-person payments is listed by 17 percent of respondents as a preferred mobile payment activity; the same percentage expresses a similar sentiment for using a mobile phone as the payment mechanism at a cash register or to use a phone as a "virtual wallet." Consumers also express some interest in using mobile payments to transfer money to friends or relatives in other countries (7 percent).

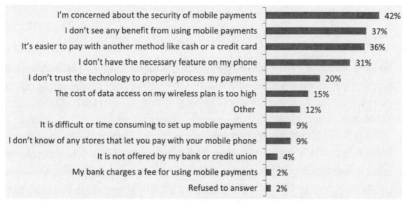

Note: This was question 39 in the survey (see Appendix 1); number of respondents was
1,780.

Figure 4. What are the main reasons why you have not used mobile payments?

Mobile Security

Two major impediments to consumers' adoption of mobile banking and mobile payment technologies are (1) concerns about security and (2) the possibility of hackers remotely accessing consumers' phones. Consumers' beliefs about whether mobile banking or mobile payment technologies are secure is correlated with their use of these technologies. Consumers who use mobile banking or mobile payments are more likely to report that it is a secure process than those who do not use mobile banking or mobile payments. For example, when consumers were asked to rate the security of text messages for mobile banking, those who are mobile banking users rate the service "very safe" (18 percent) or "somewhat safe" (42 percent). In contrast, 38 percent of non-users of mobile banking report that they "don't know" whether or not text messages for mobile banking are safe, while only 6 percent rate the service "very safe" and 27 percent rate it "somewhat safe."

The dichotomy between users and non-users of mobile banking is even more pronounced when asked about the overall security of mobile banking for protecting personal information. Two-fifths of non-users report that they do not know if it is secure, while 13 percent of this group rate mobile banking "very unsecure" and 23 percent rate the service "somewhat unsecure." Mobile banking users, however, rate mobile banking as "very safe" (18 percent) or "some-what safe" (56 percent) in maintaining their personal information.

OTHER MOBILE FINANCIAL SERVICES

There appears to be widespread interest among mobile phone users in expanding how they use mobile technology to access financial services, despite the Federal Reserve survey finding that only 21 percent of respondent mobile phone users have adopted mobile banking and only 12 percent of respondents have adopted mobile payments.

Consumers were asked to select the types of activity they would be interested in performing with their mobile phones assuming the function were made available to them (figure 5). Nearly one-half (48 percent) of consumers in the survey express an interest in using their phone to compare prices while shopping. Similarly, one-third indicate that they would like to use their mobile phones to receive location-based offers and promotions, and 31 percent indicate that they would like to receive and manage discount offers and coupons. Consumers also report that they would use their mobile phones to manage their personal finances, as 31 percent indicate that they would like to use their mobile phones to track their finances on a daily basis.

Consumers in the survey have a limited interest in using their mobile phone as a "mobile wallet": 25 percent indicate they would like to use their mobile phone to pay at the point of sale. Given the current mobile payment adoption rate of 12 percent, this would double the use of mobile payments. One fourth indicate they would use it as a membership card, and 21 percent indicate they would use it to organize and track gift cards, loyalty points, and reward points. In a related potential application of mobile technology, 23 percent of consumers indicate that they would like to use their mobile phones as a form of photo identification.

Shopping Behavior

The adoption of smartphones with barcode scanning software and Internet access has the potential to substantially alter consumer behavior in the retail environment. With this technology, consumers can quickly and easily compare prices across retailers while in store or online, or locate an item that is out of stock.

Note: This was question 46 in the survey (see Appendix 1); number of respondents was 2,002.

Figure 5. Would you like to use your mobile phone for any of the following purposes, assuming they were made available to you?

Consumers can also browse product reviews or get product specifications with little effort. Thus, consumers may become better informed about the products they purchase and find lower prices; however, the ease with which these tasks can be performed might also encourage impulse buying.

Consumers already make significant use of the Internet to inform their major purchases. A majority of respondents (58 percent) indicate that they comparison-shop online, and the same percentage say they look at product reviews before making a large purchase while at a retail store. Even though security concerns may make consumers wary of mobile devices as the payment mechanism for point-of-sale purchases, the technology can enable shopping and comparisons of products and services. About one in eight (16 percent) mobile phone users report using their mobile phone for online shopping, and nearly one-fifth of consumers with mobile phones (19 percent) say that they use their mobile phone to comparison shop while at a retail store.

Despite the relative novelty of barcode scanning applications, the Federal Reserve survey found that 12 percent of mobile phone users report using a barcode scanning application for price comparisons. One in six (16 percent) mobile phone users report using their mobile phone to browse online shopping reviews while in the store.

Many consumers who use their mobile phone to comparison-shop report that they altered their decisions as a result: 65 percent who have comparison-shopped in a store report that they changed where they made a purchase after comparing prices, and 77 percent report that they changed what they purchased as a result of reading product reviews on their mobile phone while at a retail store.

Meanwhile, as a growing number of retailers develop their capabilities in the mobile space, opportunities will arise for the use of mobile advertisements and offers. Thirty-seven percent of consumers in the survey report signing up for coupons or special offers by e-mail from retail stores in the past 12 months, and 73 percent of these consumers report having made a purchase as a result of these promotions. Moreover, 28 percent of all consumers report signing up with an online coupon or offer site such as Groupon or Living Social.

Personal Financial Management and Budgeting

Some consumers appear to be actively managing their finances using their computer and some form of personal financial management (PFM) tool. For the purposes of this survey, the Federal Reserve defined a PFM tool as a "program or website used to track your household finances (e.g., Quicken, Mint.com, Excel, or a website provided by a bank)." Slightly more than one in five consumers (21 percent) report that they, or someone in their household, use a program or website to track their household finances. Most consumers who track their finances are long-time users—42 percent report using the program or website for more than five years. The median consumer uses PFM tools about five times a month (just about once a week).

Access on a mobile phone to information about financial accounts has the potential to shape consumers' financial decisions. For example, 67 percent of mobile banking users report using their mobile phone to check account balances or available credit before making a large purchase in the past 12 months. Of those who checked their balance or available credit, 59 percent report that they decided not to buy an item because of the amount of money in their bank account or the amount of available credit.

Furthermore, some mobile phones not only allow their users to access financial accounts but also serve as PFM tools. For example, 7 percent of mobile phone users report using their mobile phone to track purchases and expenses. Among this group, 38 percent use a mobile application for expense tracking, 10 percent use a spreadsheet, 47 percent use the web browser to access a website, 12 percent send text messages, and 21 percent take notes in a notepad or word processor.

Consumers can take advantage of other financial management tools on their mobile phones, such as text alerts, to make smarter financial decisions. Alerts, reminders, and similar services provided by banks are meant to encourage positive consumer behaviors and, given the positive response to low-balance alerts, it seems that text message notices are an effective tool for encouraging consumers to engage in better financial behaviors.

One-third of mobile banking users indicate that they receive text message alerts from their bank and, out of this group, 66 percent receive "low-balance alerts" (figure 6). Nearly all report taking some action in response to getting a low-balance text alert from their bank: transferring money into the account with the low-balance (58 percent), reducing their spending (41 percent), or depositing additional money into the account (16 percent) (figure 7). Almost one-third of text message bankers (31 percent) indicate that they receive "payment due alerts," and 3 percent indicate that they receive "savings reminders."

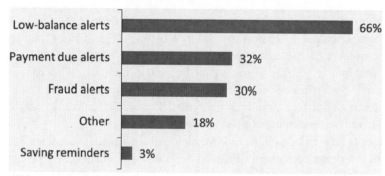

Note: This was question 74 in the survey (see Appendix 1); number of respondents was 111.

Figure 6. What kind of text alerts do you receive?

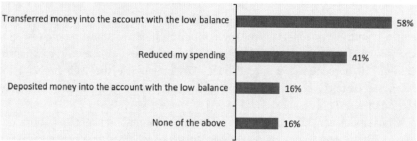

Note: This was question 75 in the survey (see **Appendix 1**); number of respondents was 78.

Figure 7. Thinking of the most recent low-balance alert you received by text message, which of the following actions did you take after receiving the alert?

Unbanked and Underbanked

As previously discussed, mobile technologies offer an opportunity to draw the unbanked and underbanked into the mainstream financial system by providing easily accessible and low-cost financial services.

Who Are the Unbanked and Underbanked?

For purposes of this report, an underbanked consumer is defined as a respondent who has a checking, savings, or money market account, but who also uses an alternative financial service such as auto title lending, payday loans, a check-cashing service, or a pay-roll card. An unbanked consumer is defined as someone who does not currently have a checking, savings, or money market account (see **box 1**).

The proportion of respondents who report being unbanked or underbanked in this survey closely tracks that found in previous national studies. In this study, about 11 percent of the U.S. adult population is currently unbanked, compared with approximately 8 percent according to the 2009 Federal Deposit Insurance Corporation (FDIC) National Survey of Unbanked and Underbanked Households and 8 percent according to the Federal Reserve's 2007 Survey of Consumer Finances (SCF).[10]

BOX 1. ALTERNATIVES TO TRADITIONAL BANKING AND FINANCIAL SERVICES

The survey included other questions on consumers' use of financial products, consumer financial behaviors, and consumer attitudes. Among those questions were ones on alternative financial services; results are reported here because of the general interest in these topics among consumer educators and community development professionals.

Over the past several decades, new financial products and services have arisen to meet the needs of consumers who may not have had their financial needs met by mainstream financial institutions, or who wanted an alternative to mainstream financial institutions.

The spreading availability and use of payday lenders, check cashers, and prepaid debit cards are prime examples of this trend.

These products and services charge fees and effective interest rates that, in some cases, can impose a significant burden on the finances of consumers and can be detrimental to consumers' long-term financial well-being.

Payday lenders typically charge consumers fees ranging from 15 to 20 percent of the loan amount for a two-week loan, which translates into an Annual Percentage Rate (APR) ranging from 390 percent to 520 percent.[1]

Among the various alternative financial products and services, use of prepaid cards is the most common in our sample—more than half (55 percent) of the respondents report using some type of prepaid card. About one out of seven respondents (15 percent) use a general purpose prepaid card, 5 percent have a government provided prepaid card, and 2 percent have a payroll card.

Why Consumers Use Payday Lenders

Eleven percent of respondents in our sample report that they or their partner/spouse have used a pay-day loan, but only 5 percent report having done so in the past 12 months. As shown in **figure A**, the main reasons for using payday loans or advances are perceptions that the borrower would not qualify for a bank loan or credit card (29 percent), that pay-day loans are easier to get than a bank loan or credit card (25 percent), and that payday loans are quicker to receive than other loans (18 percent). Few respondents indicate that the reason for using the payday lender is convenience (4 percent) or level of comfort with banks (1 percent).

Besides payday lenders and prepaid cards, the use of the other types of alternative financial services was quite rare in our sample. Only 4 percent of the overall sample reports having used a check-cashing service, auto title loan, or layaway loan in the past 12 months.

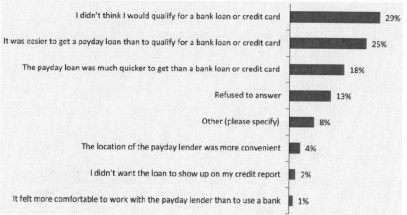

Note: This was question 6 in the survey (see Appendix 1); number of respondents was 223.

Figure A. What was the main reason for using a payday loan or payday advance service rather than a bank loan or credit card?

[1] Avery, Robert B. and Katherine A. Samolyk, 2011, *Payday Loans versus Pawn Shops: The Effects of Loan Fee Limits on Household Use*, Working Paper (www.frbsf.org/community/ conferences/2011ResearchConference/docs/2-avery-paper.pdf).

Results indicate that a further 11 percent of the U.S. population is underbanked. This rate is well below the 18 percent underbanked rate found in the FDIC study; however, the definition of underbanked here is more narrow than the FDIC's definition, as the latter includes use of services such as money orders when classifying an individual as underbanked.

Why Are Consumers Unbanked and Underbanked?

From this survey, the reasons reported for being unbanked largely mirror those found in the 2007 SCF. The most commonly cited reason is a general dislike of dealing with banks (24 percent) **(figure 8)**. Meanwhile, 23 percent report that they do not write enough checks to justify owning an account, and 13 percent indicate that the fees and service charges on an account are too high. A further 10 percent of the unbanked report that banks would not allow them to open an account.

This order of response frequency for why consumers remain unbanked tracks that found in the 2007 SCF, and the magnitudes are nearly identical. For example, 25 percent of unbanked respondents to the SCF report that they do not have a checking account because they do not like dealing with banks, and 19 percent report that they don't write enough checks to make it worthwhile.

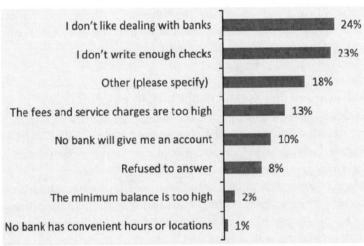

Note: This was question 3 in the survey (see Appendix 1); number of respondents was 200.

Figure 8. Please choose the reason why you do not have a checking, savings, or money market account from the following list.

Mobile Device Use by the Unbanked and Underbanked

Although 11 percent of all individuals are unbanked, they are not necessarily "unphoned." Among individuals who are unbanked, 64 percent have access to a mobile phone and 18 percent have access to a smartphone. More remarkably, 91 percent of the underbanked have a mobile phone and 57 percent have a smartphone—rates far above those for the overall population.

The Unbanked and Mobile Banking

The utilization of mobile banking among the unbanked is low, with only 10 percent reporting its use in the past 12 months. Although the concept of an unbanked mobile banking user seems counterintuitive, 32 percent of unbanked individuals do, nevertheless, report using a debit card or check card in the past 12 months. Recall that our definition of mobile banking used here includes "using a mobile phone to access your bank account, credit card account, or *other financial account* [emphasis added]." Respondents may be referring to another financial account, such as a payroll card or prepaid card, often marketed as a "debit" card.

Additionally, 19 percent of the unbanked report using a general purpose prepaid card in the past 12 months, and 9 percent report using a major credit card in the past 12 months. Mobile payment adoption among the unbanked is 12 percent, which is approximately the same as in the overall population. Given the sample size of the survey, the number of individuals who are unbanked and use mobile financial services is fewer than 20, which prevents detailed analysis of their behavior.

The Underbanked and Mobile Financial Services

The underbanked population makes substantial use of mobile financial services. Almost 29 percent of the underbanked with mobile phones report using mobile banking in the past 12 months, while 17 percent report using mobile payments.

As with all other consumers, the primary use for mobile banking among the underbanked is to check account balances, with 89 percent utilizing this service. Overall, the underbanked use mobile banking for the same purposes as the general population, with only slightly lower rates for making bill payments (20 percent relative to 26 percent) and significantly higher rates for transferring money between their accounts (55 percent relative to 42 percent).

Although the underbanked are more likely than the general population to use mobile payments, the services that they use largely mirror those of the general population with one notable exception: the underbanked are substantially more likely to make bill payments using their mobile phones. Specifically, 62 percent of underbanked mobile payments users report paying bills, with their mobile phone in the past 12 months compared with 47 percent of the overall population of mobile phone users.

CONCLUSION

The evolution of mobile technology has the potential to empower consumers and expand access to financial services for previously underserved populations. The prevalence of mobile phone access among minorities, low-income individuals, and younger generations creates the possibility of using mobile technology to expand financial inclusion to previously underserved populations.

The disproportionate use of mobile bill payment by the underbanked found in our survey is one example of how this technology can improve financial access for these groups. Mobile banking is poised for significant growth in adoption in the near future, with usage likely increasing to one in three mobile phone users by early 2013. Similarly, a significant fraction of mobile phone users appears to be interested in using phones to make mobile payments.

Consumers' perception that mobile banking and mobile payments are unsecure is currently one of the primary impediments to adoption. If consumers' perception of security issues changes—whether due to actual or perceived improvements—adoption rates may significantly increase.

APPENDIX 1. SURVEY OF CONSUMERS' FINANCIAL DECISIONMAKING USING NEW TECHNOLOGIES—QUESTIONNAIRE

Below is an exact reproduction of the survey instrument. The bracketed text are programming instructions that (1) indicate whether or not a question is single choice [SP] or multiple choice [MP] and (2) represent any skip pattern used to reach that question and which questions should be grouped together on a page. The respondents only saw the questions and response options; they did not see the program code.

[DISPLAY]

The Federal Reserve Board is interested in learning more about how people manage their finances, shop, and make payments. We are especially interested in how people use mobile phones and other technology when making financial decisions.

To begin, we are going to ask a few questions about the types of financial products and services that you use.

Banking Section

[SP]

1. Do you or does your spouse/partner currently have a checking, savings, or money market account?
   a. Yes
   b. No
   [SP]
   [IF Q1 = B]

2. Have you or your spouse/partner ever had a checking, savings, or money market account?
   a. Yes
   b. No
   [SP]
   [IF Q1 = B; shown on the same screen as Q2]

3. Please choose the **most important reason** why you don't have a checking, savings, or money market account from the following list:
   a. I don't write enough checks to make it worthwhile
   b. The minimum balance is too high
   c. I don't like dealing with banks
   d. The fees and service charges are too high
   e. No bank has convenient hours or locations
   f. No bank will give me an account
   g. Other (Please specify):**[TXT]**_____
   [SP]

4. A payday loan (also called a paycheck advance or deposit advance) is a small, short-term loan that is intended to cover your expenses until your next payday. Firms that offer these loans generally charge fees

for every $100 borrowed (for example, $15 or more). Have you or your spouse/partner ever used payday loans, paycheck advance, or deposit advance services?

a.   Yes

b.   No

[NUMBER BOX, RANGE: 0-999, IF Q4= A]

5.   How many times in the last 12 months did you or your spouse/partner use payday loan or payday advance services? In answering this question, please count a rollover of a payday loan as a new loan and also count using one pay-day loan to pay off another as separate loans.

_____ time(s) in the past 12 months

[SP, IF Q4 = A; shown on the same screen as Q5]

6.   What was the main reason for using a payday loan or payday advance services rather than a bank loan or credit card?

a.   The location of the payday lender was more convenient

b.   The payday loan was much quicker to get than a bank loan or credit card

c.   It was easier to get a payday loan than to qualify for a bank loan or credit card

d.   It felt more comfortable to work with the payday lender than to use a bank

e.   I didn't want the loan to show up on my credit report

f.   I didn't think I would qualify for a bank loan or credit card

g.   Other (Please specify):**[TXT]** _____

[DISPLAY]

A prepaid card is a card where funds are loaded or added to a card and then you access those funds with the card number or by swiping the card. It works like a debit card except that it is not connected to your bank account. A prepaid card is NOT a credit card.

There are four kinds of prepaid cards you may have seen before:

1)   Gift cards are prepaid cards that you can only use at specific stores. Examples of these include department store cards and coffee shop cards.

2)   General purpose prepaid cards are like gift cards except you can use them at many places. For example, a general purpose prepaid card can

be used at grocery stores, clothing stores, gas stations, and so forth. These cards usually have a Visa or MasterCard logo on them.

3) Payroll cards are cards used by employers instead of a paycheck or direct deposit. These cards can be used to make purchases at many stores, and to make online payments and ATM withdrawals. They usually have a Visa or MasterCard logo on them.

4) Government issued prepaid cards are given to people who receive government benefits. Examples of these cards include Direct Express and Electronic Benefit Transfer (EBT) cards. These cards can be used to make purchases or payments, but may have restrictions on what you can purchase and where you can use them. In the rest of the survey, you can click on the text of these four kinds of prepaid cards (in blue) to see their definitions.

In the rest of the survey, you can click on the text of these four kinds of prepaid cards (in blue) to see their definitions.

[PROGRAM INSTRUCTION]

DEFINITIONS. MAKE ALL INSTANCES FOR GIFT CARD, GENERAL PURPOSE PREPAID CARD, PAYROLL CARD, AND GOVERNMENT CARD **IN THE SURVEY CLICKABLE. DISPLAY A CORRESPONDING DEFINITION.** LET THE "CLICKABLE" TEXT AS A SIMPLE POPUP WINDOW THAT POPS UP IN A SMALLER SEPARATE WINDOW EVERY TIME **R** CLICK ON THE PHRASE.

Gift card. Gift cards are prepaid cards that you can only use at specific stores. Examples of these include department store cards and coffee shop cards.

General purpose prepaid card. General purpose prepaid cards are like gift cards except you can use them at many places. For example, a general purpose prepaid card can be used at grocery stores, clothing stores, gas stations, and so forth. These cards usually have a Visa or MasterCard logo on them.

Payroll card. Payroll cards are cards used by employers instead of a paycheck or direct deposit. These cards can be used to make purchases at many stores, and to make online payments and ATM withdrawals. They usually have a Visa or MasterCard logo on them.

Government issued prepaid card. Government issued prepaid cards are given to people who receive government benefits. Examples of these cards include Direct Express and Electronic Benefit Transfer (EBT) cards. These cards can be used to make purchases or payments, but may have restrictions on what you can purchase and where you can use them.

[MP]
7. Do you have any of the following types of prepaid cards?
    a. Gift card
    b. General purpose prepaid card
    c. Payroll card
    d. Government card
    e. None of the above **[Exclusive]**
    [SP, **IF Q7=A OR Q7=B OR Q7=C**]
8. Some general purpose and merchant specific prepaid cards can be reloaded with extra dollar value by the card holder. Are any of your prepaid cards reloadable?
    a. Yes
    b. No
    c. Don't know
    [SP, **IF Q8 = A**]
9. In the past 12 months, did you add money to reload any of your prepaid cards?
    a. Yes
    b. No
    [SP, **IF Q9 = A**]
10. Think about the prepaid card that you reload most often. When was the last time that you personally reloaded that prepaid card?
    a. In the past 7 days
    b. In the past 30 days
    c. In the past 90 days
    d. In the past 12 months
    e. More than 12 months ago
    f. Never
    [MP]
11. Which of the following financial products or services have you used in the past 12 months?
    a. Debit card or check card
    b. Paper check
    c. Major credit card (VISA, MasterCard, American Express, Discover)

    d.   Store-branded credit card good only at the store that issued the card
    e.   General purpose prepaid card
    f.   Auto title loan
    g.   Check cashing services
    h.   Payday loans
    i.   Layaway plan
    j.   I use none of the products listed above **[Exclusive]**
    [SP, **IF Q1 = A**]

12. **Telephone banking** is when you access your account by calling a phone number that your bank has provided. You interact with the system using either voice commands, your phone's numeric keypad, or speaking with a live customer service representative. It does not include accessing your bank using the Internet or applications on your mobile phone.

    Have you used telephone banking in the past 12 months, either with a landline phone or your mobile phone?
    a.   Yes
    b.   No
    [MP, **IF Q12 = A**]

13. Which of the following transactions have you done using telephone banking in the past 12 months?
    a.   Checked account balances or transactions
    b.   Transferred money between accounts
    c.   Paid bills
    d.   Asked a customer service question
    e.   Deposited money
    f.   Applied for a credit card or loan
    g. Other

[DISPLAY]

In this section we'll ask a few questions about your use of the Internet. Right now we are just interested in your use of the Internet on a computer (desktop, laptop, or tablet). Later on we will ask about use of the Internet on mobile phones.

    [SP]

14. Do you currently have regular access to the Internet, either at home or outside your home (i.e. school, work, public library, etc.)?
    a.   Yes

b. No
[SP, **IF Q14 = A**]

15. Where do you use the Internet the most often?
   a. At home
   b. At work
   c. At school
   d. At a library
   e. At someone else's home
   f. At an Internet café or store with Wi-Fi
   g. Other

[SP, **IF Q14 = A AND Q1 = A**]

16. **Online banking** involves checking your account balance and recent transactions, transferring money, paying bills, or conducting other related transactions with your bank or credit card company using the Internet.

   Have you used online banking on a desktop, laptop or tablet computer in the past 12 months?
   a. Yes
   b. No

[MP, **IF Q16 = A**]

17. Which of the following transactions have you done using online banking on a desktop, laptop or tablet computer in the past 12 months?
   a. Checked account balances or transactions
   b. Transferred money between accounts
   c. Paid bills
   d. Asked a customer service question
   e. Deposited money
   f. Applied for a credit card or loan
   g. Managed investments (i.e. bought and sold stock or mutual funds)
   h. Other

Screener Question on Mobile Phone Usage
[DISPLAY]

In this section we would like to ask you about your use of mobile phones (cell phones). You may be able to use your mobile phone to check bank account balances, transfer funds, pay bills, or carry out other financial transactions. Mobile phones are also being used to make payments to stores, for parking, or to another person. Mobile phones can help you shop by comparing prices or looking up product reviews while you are in the store.

[SP, PROMPT, TERMINATE IF SKIPPED]

18. Do you own or have regular access to a mobile phone (cell phone)?
    a. Yes → **[MOBILE = "YES"]**
    b. No → **[MOBILE = "NO"]**
    DOV: MOBILE
1: "YES"
2: "NO" [SP]
    [MOBILE = "YES"]

19. A smartphone is a mobile phone with features that may enable it to access the web, send e-mails, and interact with computers. Smartphones include the iPhone, BlackBerrys, as well as Android and Windows Mobile powered devices.
    Is your mobile phone a smart phone?
    a. Yes
    b. No
    [SP]
    [IF Q19 = A]

20. Which type of smart phone do you have?
    a. Android
    b. Blackberry
    c. iPhone
    d. Windows Mobile
    e. Other
    f. Don't know
    [SP]
    [IF Q19 = A; shown on the same screen as Q20]

21. When was the last time that you used the Internet on your mobile phone?
    a. In the past 7 days
    b. In the past 30 days
    c. In the past 90 days
    d. In the past 12 months
    e. More than 12 months ago
    f. Never

Mobile Banking Users

[MOBILE = "YES"]
[DISPLAY]

Mobile banking uses a mobile phone to access your bank account, credit card account, or other financial account. This can be done either by accessing your bank's web page through the web browser on your mobile phone, via text messaging, or by using an application downloaded to your mobile phone.
[SP]
22. Have you used mobile banking in the past 12 months?
    a. Yes
    b. No
    [SP]
    [IF Q22 = B]

23. Do you plan to use mobile banking in the next 12 months?
    a. Definitely will use
    b. Probably will use
    c. Probably will not use
    d. Definitely will not use
    [SP]
    [IF Q23 = C OR Q23 = D]

24. Do you think you will ever use mobile banking?
    a. Definitely will use
    b. Probably will use
    c. Probably will not use
    d. Definitely will not use
    [MP]
    [IF Q22 = A]

25. Using your mobile phone, have you done any of the following in the past 12 months?
    a. Downloaded your bank's mobile banking application on your mobile phone
    b. Checked an account balance or checked recent transactions
    c. Made a bill payment using your bank's online banking website or banking application

    d.   Received a text message alert from your bank

    e.   Transferred money between two accounts

    f.   Deposited a check to your account using your phone's camera

    g.   Located the closest in-network ATM for your bank

    h.   Managed your investments (i.e. bought and sold stock or mutual funds)

    i.   Other banking-related activities (Please specify):[**TXT**]____

    [IF Q22 = A; NUMBER BOX; RANGE: 0-999; shown on the same screen as Q25]

26. In a typical month, how many times do you personally use mobile banking? If never please enter "0". _____times

    [SP]

    [IF Q22 = A; shown on the same screen as Q25]

27. Overall, how satisfied are you with your mobile banking experiences?

    a.   Very satisfied

    b.   Somewhat satisfied

    c.   Somewhat dissatisfied

    d.   Very dissatisfied

    [MP, ONLY TWO CHOICES PERMITTED, IF MORE THAN TWO, PROMPT "PLEASE SELECT ONLY TWO CHOICES."]

    [IF Q27 = C OR Q27 = D]

28. What are the top two reasons you are dissatisfied with your mobile banking experiences?

    a.   I am concerned about my personal information being disclosed or have had personal information disclosed as a result of mobile banking

    b.   Applications and/or websites for mobile banking are too complicated to use

    c.   I have had problems getting the websites or applications to work properly

    d.   Banking on my mobile phone takes too long

    e.   It is too difficult to see on my mobile phone's screen

    f.   The transactions I want to execute are not available

    g.   Other (Please specify):[**TXT**] _____

Mobile Payments Users

[MOBILE = "YES"]
[DISPLAY]

Mobile payments are purchases, bill payments, charitable donations, payments to another person, or any other payments made using a mobile phone. You can do this either by accessing a web page through the web browser on your mobile device, by sending a text message (SMS), or by using a downloadable application on your mobile device. The amount of the payment may be applied to your phone bill (for example Red Cross text message donation), charged to your credit card, or withdrawn directly from your bank account.
[SP]
29. Have you made a mobile payment in the past 12 months?
    a. Yes
    b. No
[MP]
[IF Q29 = A]

30. Using your mobile phone, have you done any of the following in the past 12 months?
    a. Transferred money directly to another person's bank, credit card or Pay-pal account (i.e. friend, relative)
    b. Received money from another person using my mobile phone
    c. Waved or tapped my mobile phone at the cash register to pay for a purchase
    d. Paid bills online (excluding payments made directly from your bank website or application)
    e. Made a charitable donation by text message
    f. Transferred money to friends or family in another country
    g. Used my mobile phone as a "virtual wallet" to replace the cards I previously carried in my wallet
    h. Made online purchases
    i. None of the above [**Exclusive**]
[MP]
[IF Q30 = A to H]

31. Do you make your mobile payments using a credit card number, your bank account, adding the charge to your phone bill, or through a service such as Paypal, Google Wallet, or iTunes, which indirectly charges your credit card or bank account? (Select all that apply)
    a. Credit card, debit card or prepaid card number
    b. Bank account
    c. Charged to your phone bill
    d. Paypal, Google Wallet, iTunes, etc.
    e. Other (Please specify):[TXT] _____
    [MP]
    [IF Q29 = A]

32. Have you used any of the following methods to make or receive mobile payments in the past 12 months?
    a. Used a text message to make or receive a mobile payment
    b. Waved or tapped my mobile phone at the cash register or other payment sensor
    c. Scanned a barcode using your mobile phone to make a mobile payment
    d. Used your mobile phone's web browser to make or receive a mobile payment
    e. Used a downloadable app to make or receive a mobile payment f. None of the above [Exclusive]
    [IF Q29 = A; NUMBER BOX; RANGE: 0-99; shown on the same screen as Q32]

33. In a typical month, how many times do you use your mobile phone to make payments? If never please enter "0". _____times
    [SP]
    [IF Q29 = A; shown on the same screen as Q32]

34. Overall, how satisfied are you with your mobile payment experiences?
    a. Very satisfied
    b. Somewhat satisfied
    c. Somewhat dissatisfied
    d. Very dissatisfied
    [MP, ONLY TWO CHOICES PERMITTED, IF MORE THAN TWO, PROMPT "PLEASE SELECT ONLY TWO CHOICES."]

[IF Q34 = C OR Q34 = D]

35. What are the top two reasons you are dissatisfied with your mobile payment experiences? (Select only two choices)
    a. I am concerned about my personal information being disclosed or have had personal information disclosed as a result of making mobile payments
    b. I find that applications and/or websites for mobile payments are too complicated to use
    c. I have had problems getting the websites or applications to work properly
    d. It is too difficult to see on my mobile phone's screen
    e. Making mobile payments takes too long
    f. Making mobile payments is much more complicated than using another payment method
    g. Merchants don't generally accept mobile payments

    h. The transactions I want to execute are not available
    i. Other (Please specify):**[TXT]** _____

Non-Mobile Banking Users

[IF Q22 = B]
[DISPLAY]

We would like to ask you about some of your reasons for not using mobile banking

[MP]
[IF Q22 = B]
36. You indicated that you do not currently use mobile banking. What are the main reasons why you have decided not to use mobile banking?
    a. I'm concerned about the security of mobile banking
    b. My banking needs are being met without mobile banking
    c. The cost of data access on my wireless plan is too high
    d. It is too difficult to see on my mobile phone's screen e. It is not offered by my bank or credit union
    f. My bank charges a fee for using mobile banking

g. I don't trust the technology to properly process my banking transactions
h. I don't have a banking account with which to use mobile banking
i.   It's difficult or time consuming to set up mobile banking
j. Other (Please specify):[TXT] _____
[SP]
[IF Q36 = A]

37. You mentioned that security was one of your top concerns with mobile banking. What security aspects are you most concerned with?
a. Hackers gaining access to my phone remotely
b. Someone intercepting my calls or data
c. Losing my phone or having my phone stolen
d. Malware or viruses being installed on my phone
e. Other (Please specify):[TXT] _____
[MP]
[IF Q22 = B]

38. Assuming that any concerns you have about mobile banking were addressed, which of the following activities would you be interested in doing with your mobile phone?
a. Download your bank's mobile banking application on your mobile phone
b. Check an account balance or check recent transactions
c. Make a bill payment using your bank's online banking website or banking application
d. Receive text message alerts from your bank
e. Transfer money between two accounts
f. Other banking-related activities (Please specify):[TXT] _____

Non-Mobile Payments Users

[IF Q29 = B]
[DISPLAY; shown on the same page as 39]

We would like to ask you about some of your reasons for not using mobile payments

[MP]
[IF Q29 = B]

39. You indicated that you do not use mobile payments. What are the main reasons why you have decided not to use mobile payments?
    a. I'm concerned about the security of mobile payments
    b. It's easier to pay with another method like cash or a credit card
    c. I don't see any benefit from using mobile payments
    d. I don't know of any stores that let you pay with your mobile phone
    e. I don't have the necessary feature on my phone
    f. The cost of data access on my wireless plan is too high
    g. It is not offered by my bank or credit union
    h. My bank charges a fee for using mobile payments
    i. I don't trust the technology to properly process my payments
    j. It's difficult or time consuming to set up mobile payments
    k. Other (Please specify):[**TXT**] _____

[SP]
[IF Q39 = A]

40. You mentioned that security was one of your top concerns with mobile payments. What security aspect are you most concerned with?
    a. Hackers gaining access to my phone remotely
    b. Someone intercepting my payment information or other data
    c. Losing my phone or having my phone stolen
    d. Malware or viruses being installed on my phone
    e. Other (Please specify):[**TXT**] _____

[MP]
[IF Q29 = B]

41. Assuming that the reason(s) why you do not currently use mobile payments was addressed, which of the following activities would you be interested in doing with your mobile phone?
    a. Making payments directly to another person (i.e. friend, relative)
    b. Waving or tapping my mobile phone at the cash register to pay for a purchase
    c. Paying bills online
    d. Transferring money to friends or family in another country
    e. Using your mobile phone as a "virtual wallet" to replace all the cards you currently carry in your wallet

f.   Buying goods or services online

g.   Receiving/using coupons on your phone

h.   Receiving specials and discount offers based on your location

i. Other payment-related activities (Please specify):[TXT] _____

[SP]

[IF Q1 = B]

Mobile Financial Services Security Questions

[MOBILE = "YES" FOR QUESTIONS 42 THROUGH 47]

[DISPLAY, SHOW IT ON THE SAME SCREEN WITH Q42 TO Q45]

Please rate the level of security of each of the following four methods for mobile banking from Very Safe to Very Unsafe.

[SP]

42. SMS (text messaging)
    a.   Very safe
    b.   Somewhat safe
    c.   Somewhat unsafe
    d.   Very unsafe
    e.   Don't know
    [SP]

43. Mobile browser similar to the way you access the Internet on your PC
    a.   Very safe
    b.   Somewhat safe
    c.   Somewhat unsafe
    d.   Very unsafe
    e.   Don't know
    [SP]

44. Application downloaded from your phone's mobile app store
    a.   Very safe
    b.   Somewhat safe
    c.   Somewhat unsafe
    d.   Very unsafe
    e.   Don't know
    [SP]

45. How would you currently rate the overall security of mobile banking for protecting your personal information?

a. Very safe
b. Somewhat safe
c. Somewhat unsafe
d. Very unsafe
e. Don't know
[MP]

46. Would you like to use your mobile phone for any of the following purposes, assuming they were made available to you?
   a. Buy things at the point of sale
   b. Track your finances on a daily basis
   c. Organize and track gift cards, loyalty and reward points
   d. Compare prices when shopping
   e. As a ticket for buses, trains, or subways f. As a key to enter your house
   g. Purchase tickets to events
   h. As a membership card (such as museums, gym, etc.)
   i. To receive and manage discount offers and coupons
   j. To receive offers and promotions based on where you are (i.e. You walk into a store and a coupon appears on your mobile phone for a product sold there)
   k. As a form of photo identification
   [SP]

47. Banks can offer a service whereby checks to be deposited are photographed using your camera phone and the image is sent over the mobile Internet during a mobile banking session so that the bank can deposit the funds into your account without you having to present the physical check. The bank then sends a notification acknowledging receipt of the deposit.
   If your bank offered this service, how likely would you be to use it?
   a. I already use it
   b. Very likely
   c. Somewhat likely
   d. Somewhat unlikely
   e. Very unlikely

Shopping Behavior Questions
[ASKED OF EVERYONE]
[DISPLAY]

In this section we would like to ask you about your shopping habits.

[SP]
[IF Q14 = A]

48. Before going to a retail store to make a large purchase, do you generally compare prices online?
    a. Yes
    b. No
    [SP]
    [IF Q14 = A; shown on the same screen as Q48]

49. Before going to a retail store to make a large purchase, do you generally look at product reviews online?
    a. Yes
    b. No
    [SP]
    [IF MOBILE = "YES"]

50. Online shopping is when you go to a merchant's website through your web browser or an application and make a purchase. Have you ever used your mobile phone for online shopping?
    a. Yes
    b. No
    [SP]
    [IF MOBILE = "YES"; shown on the same screen as Q50]

51. Have you ever used your mobile phone to comparison shop over the Internet while at a retail store?
    a. Yes
    b. No
    [SP]
    [IF MOBILE = "YES"; shown on the same screen as Q50]
52. Have you ever used a barcode scanning application on your mobile phone while shopping at a retail store to find the best price for an item?
    a. Yes
    b. No
    [SP]
    [IF Q51 = A OR Q52 = A]

53. Has using your mobile phone to compare prices while you were shopping at a retail store ever changed where you made your purchase?
    a. Yes
    b. No
    [SP]
    [IF MOBILE = "YES"]

54. Have you ever used your mobile phone to browse product reviews while shopping at a retail store?
    a. Yes
    b. No
    [SP]
    [IF Q54 = A]

55. Has reading product reviews on your mobile phone while shopping at a retail store ever changed which item you ended up purchasing?
    a. Yes
    b. No
    [SP]
    [IF Q22 = A]

56. In the past 12 months, have you used your mobile phone to check your account balance or available credit before making a large purchase?
    a. Yes
    b. No
    [SP]
    [IF Q56 = A]

57. Thinking of the most recent time that you used your mobile phone to check your account balance or available credit before making a large purchase did you decide not to buy that particular item because of the amount of money left in your account or the amount of your available credit?
    a. Yes
    b. No
    [SP]
    [ASKED OF EVERYONE]

58. Have you signed up to receive coupons or special offers by e-mail from retail stores in the past 12 months?
    a. Yes
    b. No
    [SP]
    [IF Q58 = A]

59. Have you made a purchase as a result of receiving one of these coupons or special offers?
    a. Yes
    b. No
    [SP]
    [ASKED OF EVERYONE]

60. Have you ever signed up to receive coupons/offers from a website such as Group on or Living Social?
    a. Yes
    b. No
    [SP]
    [IF Q60 = A]

61. Have you ever used a coupon from a website such as Groupon or Living Social?
    a. Yes
    b. No

Payments Choice
[MOBILE = "YES"]
[DISPLAY]
In this section we would like to ask about your thoughts on some of the new mobile financial service technologies.
    [SP]
    [MOBILE = "YES"]

62. New **mobile** "contactless" payments are becoming available from some banks, credit card companies, and transit operators. These let consumers "tap" or wave their mobile phone at a terminal instead of swiping a card.

If you were offered the option of using this service, how likely would you be to use it?

a. I already use it
b. Very likely
c. Somewhat likely
d. Somewhat unlikely
e. Very unlikely

[SP]

[MOBILE = "YES"; shown on the same screen as Q62]

63. How likely do you think it is that mobile contactless payments will become a major form of payment in the next five years?

a. Very likely
b. Somewhat likely
c. Somewhat unlikely
d. Very unlikely
e. Don't know

Financial Management (Saving, Budgeting) Questions
[ASKED OF EVERYONE]
[DISPLAY, SHOW IT ON THE SAME SCREEN WITH Q64 TO Q67]

In order to help us to understand your role in the financial activities of your household, please rank how much responsibility you have for the following four financial tasks

[SP]

64. Maintaining the household budget and managing household income

a. None or almost none
b. Some
c. Shared equally with other household members
d. Most
e. All or almost all

[SP]

65. Paying monthly bills (rent or mortgage, utilities, cell phone, etc.)

a. None or almost none
b. Some
c. Shared equally with other household members
d. Most

e.   All or almost all
[SP]

66. Shopping for household goods and groceries
    a.   None or almost none
    b.   Some
    c.   Shared equally with other household members
    d.   Most
    e.   All or almost all
    [SP]

67. Making decisions about saving and investments (whether to save, how much to save, where to invest)
    a.   None or almost none
    b.   Some
    c.   Shared equally with other household members
    d.   Most
    e.   All or almost all
    [SP]

68. Do you or anyone in your household use a program or website to track your household finances (for example, Quicken, Mint.com, Excel, or a website provided by your bank)?
    a.   Yes
    b.   No
    [SP, IF Q68= A]

69. How long have you been using this program or website to manage your house-hold finances?
    a.   Less than a year
    b.   One to two years
    c.   Three to five years
    d.   More than five years
    [IF Q68= A; NUMBER BOX; RANGE: 0-999; shown on the same screen as Q69]

70. In a typical month, how often do you or another household member use this program or website? (If never please enter "0") ___times
    [SP, IF MOBILE= "YES"]

71. Do you use your mobile phone to track purchases and expenses?
    a.   Yes

b.   No
[MP, IF Q71= A]

72. What method(s) do you use to track purchases and expenses on your mobile phone?
    a.   A mobile application for expense tracking
    b.   A spreadsheet
    c.   Online (using the web browser to access a website)
    d.   Send text messages
    e.   Take notes in a notepad or word processor
    [IF Q71= A; NUMBER BOX; RANGE: 0-999; shown on the same screen as Q72]

73. In a typical month, how often do you use your mobile phone to track purchases and expenses? (If never please enter "0") _____times
    [MP, IF Q25= D]

74. You previously mentioned that you receive text alerts from your bank. What kind of text alerts do you receive?
    a.   Low-balance alerts
    b.   Payment due alerts
    c.   Saving reminders
    d.   Fraud alerts
    e.   Other (Please specify): **[TXT]**_____

    [MP, IF Q74= A]

75. Thinking of the most recent low-balance alert you received by text message, which of the following actions did you take after receiving the alert?
    a.   Transferred money into the account with the low-balance
    b.   Deposited money into the account with the low-balance
    c.   Reduced my spending
    d.   None of the above **[Exclusive]**
    [SP, IF Q74= B]

76. Has receiving payment due alerts improved your ability to pay your bills on time?
    a.   Yes, by a lot

b.   Yes, by a little

c.   No

Financial Literacy Questions
[ASKED OF EVERYONE]

[SP]
77. Imagine that the interest rate on your savings account was 1% per year and inflation was 2% per year. After 1 year, how much would you be able to buy with the money in this account?
   a.   More than today
   b.   Exactly the same
   c.   Less than today
   [SP; shown on the same screen as Q77]

78. Considering a long time period (for example, 10 or 20 years), which asset normally gives the highest return?
   a.   Savings accounts
   b.   U.S. Government bonds
   c.   Stocks
   [SP; shown on the same screen as Q77]

79. If an investor who only owns two stocks right now decides to instead spread their money among many different assets (i.e. more stocks, add bonds, add real estate), their risk of losing money on their entire portfolio will:
   a.   Increase
   b.   Decrease
   c.   Stay the same
   [SP]

80. If you were to invest $1000 in a stock mutual fund for a year, it would be possible to have less than $1000 when you withdraw your money.
   a.   True
   b.   False
   [SP; shown on the same screen as Q80]

81. Suppose you owe $1,000 on a loan and the interest rate you are charged is 10% per year compounded annually. If you didn't make

any payments on this loan, at this interest rate, how many years would it take for the amount you owe to double?

a.   Less than 2 years
b.   Between 2 and 5 years
c.   5 to 9 years
d.   10 years or more

[MP]

82. Imagine that your car breaks down and requires $400 worth of repairs in order to drive again. **Based on your current financial situation, how would you pay for this expense?** If you would use more than one method to cover this expense please select all that apply.

a.   Put it on my credit card
b.   With the money currently in my checking account
c.   By taking money out of my savings
d.   Using money from a bank loan, line of credit, or overdraft
e.   By borrowing from a friend or family member
f.   Using a payday loan or deposit advance
g.   By pawning something
h.   Other (Please specify): **[TXT]** _____

Risk Aversion Questions
[ASKED OF EVERYONE]

[SP]

83. Which of the following statements comes closest to describing the amount of financial risk that you are willing to take when you save or make investments?

a.   Take substantial financial risks expecting to earn substantial returns
b.   Take above average financial risks expecting to earn above average returns
c.   Take average financial risks expecting to earn average returns
d.   Not willing to take any financial risks

[SP]

84. Suppose that you are the only income earner in the family, and you have a good job guaranteed to give you your current income every year for life. You are given the opportunity to take a new and equally good job, with a 50–50 chance that it will double your income and a

50–50 chance that it will cut your income by one-third (33 percent). Would you take the new job?

a. Yes

b. No

[SP]

[IF Q84 = A]

85. Now suppose that the chances were 50–50 that it would double your income and 50–50 that it would cut your income by half (50 percent). Would you still take the new job?

a. Yes

b. No

[SP]

[IF Q84 = B]

86. Now suppose that the chances were 50–50 that it would double your income and 50–50 that it would cut your income by one-fifth (20 percent). Would you now take the new job?

a. Yes

b. No

APPENDIX 2.
CONSUMER RESPONSES TO
SURVEY QUESTIONNAIRE

Table B.1. Do you or does your spouse/partner currently have a checking, savings, or money market account?

Percent, except as noted	
Q1	
Yes	88.7
No	10.8
Refused to answer	0.5
Number of respondents	**2,290**

Table B.2. Have you or your spouse/partner ever had a checking, savings, or money market account?

Percent, except as noted	
Q2	
Yes	36.9
No	58.9
Refused to answer	4.2
Number of respondents	**200**

Table B.3. Please choose the most important reason why you don't have a checking, savings, or money market account from the following list

Percent, except as noted	
Q3	
I don't write enough checks to make it worthwhile	23.5
The minimum balance is too high	2.2
I don't like dealing with banks	24.2
The fees and service charges are too high	13.3
No bank has convenient hours or locations	0.6
No bank will give me an account	10.2
Other	17.8
Refused to answer	8.1
Number of respondents	**200**

Table B.4. Have you or your spouse/partner ever used payday loans, paycheck advance, or deposit advance services?

Percent, except as noted	
Q4	
Yes	11.2
No	88.1
Refused to answer	0.8
Number of respondents	**2,290**

Table B.5. How many times in the last 12 months did you or your spouse/partner use payday loan or payday advance services? In answering this question, please count a rollover of a payday loan as a new loan and also count using one payday loan to pay off another as separate loans

Percent, except as noted	
Q5	
0	44.9
1	13.8
2	11.6
3	6.3
4	3.9
5	5.3
6	3.1
7	0.3
8	0.9
9	0.1
10	2.6
12	2.1
16	0.5
20	0.5
24	0.3
40	0.6
Refused to answer	3.1
Number of respondents	**223**

Table B.6. What was the main reason for using a payday loan or payday advance service rather than a bank loan or credit card?

Percent, except as noted	
Q6	
The location of the payday lender was more convenient	3.6
The payday loan was much quicker to get than a bank loan or credit card	17.7
It was easier to get a payday loan than to qualify for a bank loan or credit card	24.9
It felt more comfortable to work with the payday lender than to use a bank	1.2
I didn't want the loan to show up on my credit report	2.1
I didn't think I would qualify for a bank loan or credit card	29.2
Other	8
Refused to answer	13.4
Number of respondents	**223**

**Table B.7. Do you have any of the following
types of prepaid cards?**

Percent, except as noted	
Q7	
Gift card	48
General purpose prepaid card	14.5
Payroll card	1.7
Government card	4.8
None of the above	45.4
Refused to answer	0.4
Number of respondents	**2,290**

**Table B.8. Some general purpose and merchant specific prepaid cards can
be reloaded with extra dollar value by the cardholder.
Are any of your prepaid cards reloadable?**

Percent, except as noted	
Q8	
Yes	44.7
No	30.4
Don't know	24.5
Refused to answer	0.4
Number of respondents	**1,228**

**Table B.9. In the past 12 months,
did you add money to reload any of your prepaid cards?**

Percent, except as noted	
Q9	
Yes	40.3
No	59.7
Number of respondents	**498**

Table B.10. Think about the prepaid card that you reload most often. When was the last time that you personally reloaded that prepaid card?

Percent, except as noted	
Q10	
In the past 7 days	21.2
In the past 30 days	41.1
In the past 90 days	20
In the past 12 months	17.1
More than 12 months ago	0.6
Never	0.1
Number of respondents	**207**

Table B.11. Which of the following financial products or services have you used in the past 12 months?

Percent, except as noted	
Q11	
Debit card or check	69
Paper check	66.7
Major credit card	60.2
Store-branded credit card good only at the store that issued the card	30.2
General purpose prepaid card	18.6
Auto title loan	3.5
Check cashing service	4.1
Payday loan	3.3
Layaway plan	3.8
None of the above	7.2
Refused to answer	0.6
Number of respondents	**2,290**

Table B.12. Have you used telephone banking in the past 12 months, either with a landline phone or your mobile phone?

Percent, except as noted	
Q12	
Yes	33.3
No	66.3
Refused to answer	0.4
Number of respondents	**2,079**

Table B.13. Which of the following transactions have you performed using telephone banking in the past 12 months?

Percent, except as noted	
Q13	
Checked account balances or transactions	78.1
Transferred money between accounts	31.3
Paid bills	29.8
Asked a customer service question	44
Deposited money	4.8
Applied for a credit card or loan	2.4
Other	2.7
Refused to answer	0.3
Number of respondents	**653**

Table B.14. Do you currently have regular access to the Internet, either at home or outside your home (i.e., school, work, public library)?

Percent, except as noted	
Q14	
Yes	95.4
No	4.3
Refused to answer	0.4
Number of respondents	**2,290**

Table B.15. Where do you use the Internet the most often?

Percent, except as noted	
Q15	
At home	80.8
At work	14.8
At school	0.8
At a library	1.7
At someone else's home	1
At an Internet café or store with Wi-Fi	0.3
Other	0.3
Refused to answer	0.2
Number of respondents	**2,189**

Table B.16. Have you used online banking on a desktop, laptop, or tablet computer in the past 12 months?

Percent, except as noted	
Q16	
Yes	67.7
No	31.9
Refused to answer	0.5
Number of respondents	**2,011**

Table B.17. Which of the following transactions have you done using online banking on a desktop, laptop, or tablet computer in the past 12 months?

Percent, except as noted	
Q17	
Checked account balances or transactions	95.8
Transferred money between accounts	67.6
Paid bills	73.1
Asked a customer service question	11.8
Deposited money	11.9
Applied for a credit card or loan	8
Managed investments (i.e., bought and sold stock or mutual funds)	8.8
Other	0.8
Refused to answer	0.4
Number of respondents	**1,358**

Table B.18. Do you own or have regular access to a mobile phone (cell phone)?

Percent, except as noted	
Q18	
Yes	87.1
No	12.9
Number of respondents	**2,290**

Table B.19. Is your mobile phone a smartphone?

Percent, except as noted	
Q19	
Yes	43.9
No	55.9
Refused to answer	0.2
Number of respondents	**2,002**

Table B.20. Which type of smartphone do you have?

Percent, except as noted	
Q20	
Android	43.4
BlackBerry	13.1
iPhone	30.1
Windows Mobile	1.2
Other	7.7
Don't know	3.9
Refused to answer	0.5
Number of respondents	**836**

Table B.21. When was the last time that you used the Internet on your mobile phone?

Percent, except as noted	
Q21	
In the past 7 days	83.6
In the past 30 days	5.5
In the past 90 days	2.4
In the past 12 months	1.6
More than 12 months ago	0.3
Never	6.5
Refused to answer	0.1
Number of respondents	**836**

Table B.22. Have you used mobile banking in the past 12 months?

Percent, except as noted	
Q22	
Yes	20.9
No	78.9
Refused to answer	0.2
Number of respondents	**2,002**

Table B.23. Do you plan to use mobile banking in the next 12 months?

Percent, except as noted Percent, except as noted	
Q23	
Definitely will use	0.8
Probably will use	10.4
Probably will not use	39.6
Definitely will not use	48.6
Refused to answer	0.5
Number of respondents	**1,626**

Table B.24. Do you think you will ever use mobile banking?

Percent, except as noted	
Q24	
Definitely will use	0.6
Probably will use	16.4
Probably will not use	45.4
Definitely will not use	36.9
Refused to answer	0.8
Number of respondents	**1,449**

Table B.25. Using your mobile phone, have you done any of the following in the past 12 months?

Percent, except as noted	
Q25	
Downloaded your s mobile banking application on your mobile phone	48.1
Checked an account balance or checked recent transactions	90.1
Made a bill payment using your bank's online banking website or banking application	25.7
Received a text message alert from your bank	33.4

Percent, except as noted	
Q25	
Transferred money between two accounts	41.7
Deposited a check to your account using your phone's camera	10.6
Located the closest in-network ATM for your bank	20.7
Managed your investments (i.e., bought and sold stock or mutual funds)	2.2
Other banking-related activities	1
Refused to answer	3
Number of respondents	372

Table B.26. In a typical month, how many times do you personally use mobile banking?

Percent, except as noted	
Q26	
0	6
1	11.7
2	12.6
3	10.7
4	8.8
5	9.7
6	3.6
7	2.1
8	2.4
9	0.5
10	9.5
12	0.6
15	4.3
16	0.8
20	9.5
25	0.8
30	3.1
50	0.3
60	0.6
Refused to answer	2.4
Number of respondents	**372**

Table B.27. Overall, how satisfied are you with your mobile banking experiences?

Percent, except as noted	
Q27	
Very satisfied	61.7
Somewhat satisfied	32.3
Somewhat dissatisfied	2.1
Very dissatisfied	1.1
Refused to answer	2.9
Number of respondents	**372**

Table B.28. What are the top two reasons you are dissatisfied with your mobile banking experience?

Frequency, except as noted	
Q28	
I am concerned about my personal information being disclosed	5
I have had problems getting the websites or applications to work properly	4
Banking on my mobile phone takes too long	6
It is too difficult to see on my mobile phone's screen	3
The transactions I want to execute are not available	3
Other	7
Number of respondents	14

Table B.29. Have you made a mobile payment in the past 12 months?

Percent, except as noted	
Q29	
Yes	12.3
No	87.3
Refused to answer	0.4
Number of respondents	**2,002**

Table B.30. Using your mobile phone, have you done any of the following in the past 12 months?

Percent, except as noted	
Q30	
Transferred money directly to another person's bank, credit card, or paypal account	20.5
Received money from another person using my mobile phone	7.9
Waved or tapped my mobile phone at the cash register to pay for a purchase	2.4
Paid bills online (excluding payments made directly from your bank website or application	47.1
Made a charitable donation via text message	5.1
Transferred money to friends or family in another country	0.2
Used my mobile phone as a "virtual wallet" to replace the cards I previously carried in my wallet	0.2
Made online purchases	36
None of the above	23
Refused to answer	0.4
Number of respondents	**213**

Table B.31. Do you make your mobile payments using a credit card number, your bank account, adding the charge to your phone bill, or through a service such as Paypal, Google Wallet, or iTunes, that indirectly charges your credit card or bank account?

Percent, except as noted	
Q31	
Credit card, debit card, or prepaid card	66.4
Bank account	45.4
Charged to your phone bill	8.4
Paypal, Google Wallet, iTunes, etc.	21.9
Other	3.9
Number of respondents	**161**

Table B.32. Have you used any of the following methods to make or receive mobile payments in the past 12 months?

Percent, except as noted	
Q32	
Used a text message to make or receive a mobile payment	16.2
Waved or tapped my mobile phone at the cash register or other payment sensor	1.3
Scanned a barcode using your mobile phone to make a mobile payment	1
Used your mobile phone's web browser to make or receive a mobile payment	23
Used a downloadable app to make or receive a mobile payment	21
None of the above	45
Refused to answer	5.4
Number of respondents	**213**

Table B.33. In a typical month, how many times do you use your mobile phone to make payments?

Percent, except as noted	
Q33	
0	25
1	34.4
2	12.7
3	6.6
4	4.8
5	4.4
6	1.9
7	0.1
8	0.3
9	1.3
10	1.5
12	0.1
14	0.2
15	0.4
24	0.6
Refused to answer	5.7
Number of respondents	**213**

Table B.34. Overall, how satisfied are you with your mobile payment experiences?

Percent, except as noted	
Q34	
Very satisfied	55.2
Somewhat satisfied	32.6
Somewhat dissatisfied	1.5
Very dissatisfied	3.3
Refused to answer	7.4
Number of respondents	**213**

Table B.35. What are the top two reasons you are dissatisfied with your mobile payment experiences?

Frequency, except as noted	
Q35	
I am concerned about my personal information being disclosed or have had personal information disclosed	10
I find that applications and/or websites for mobile payments are too complicated to use	2
I have had problems getting the websites or applications to work properly	4
Making mobile payments takes too long	1
Making mobile payments is much more complicated than using another payment method	6
It is too difficult to see on my mobile phone's screen	2
Merchants don't generally accept mobile payments	2
Other	1
Number of respondents	**14**

Table B.36. You indicated that you do not use mobile banking. What are the main reasons why you have decided not to use mobile banking?

Percent, except as noted	
Q36	
I am concerned about the security of mobile banking	48
My banking needs are being met without mobile banking	57.5
The cost of data access on my wireless plan is too high	18.3
It is too difficult to see on my mobile phone's screen	16.6

Table B.36. (Continued)

Percent, except as noted	
Q36	
It is not offered by my bank or credit union	2.7
My bank charges a fee for using mobile banking	2.2
I don't trust the technology to properly process my banking transactions	21.8
I don't have a banking account with which to use mobile banking	8.8
It is difficult or time consuming to set up mobile banking	9.5
Other	12.6
Refused to answer	0.6
Number of respondents	**1626**

Table B.37. You mentioned that security was one of your top concerns with mobile banking. What security aspects are you most concerned with?

Percent, except as noted	
Q37	
Hackers gaining access to my phone remotely	54.3
Someone intercepting my calls or data	18.1
Losing my phone or having my phone stolen	19.3
Malware or viruses being installed on my phone	4.8
Other	3.3
Refused to answer	0.2
Number of respondents	**798**

Table B.38. Assuming that any concerns you have about mobile banking were addressed, which of the following activities would you be interested in performing with your mobile phone?

Percent, except as noted	
Q38	
Download your s mobile banking application on your mobile phone	16.6
Check an account balance or check recent transactions	55.4
Make a bill payment using your bank's online banking website or banking application	23.7
Receive text message alerts from your bank	30.2
Transfer money between two accounts	24.5
Other banking-related activities	9

Percent, except as noted	
Q38	
Refused to answer	12.6
Number of respondents	**1,626**

Table B.39. You indicated that you do not use mobile payments. What are the main reasons you have decided not to use mobile payments?

Percent, except as noted	
Q39	
I am concerned about the security of mobile payments	41.5
It is easier to pay with another method like cash or a credit card	36
I don't see any benefit from using mobile payments	36.7
I don't know of any stores that let you pay with your mobile phone	9
I t have the necessary feature on my phone	30.8
The cost of data access on my wireless plan is too high	15.3
It is not offered by my bank or credit union	4.3
My bank charges a fee for using mobile payments	1.9
I don't trust the technology to properly process my payments	19.7
It is difficult or time consuming to set up mobile payments	9.1
Other	12.4
Refused to answer	1.7
Number of respondents	**1,780**

Table B.40. You mentioned that security was one of your top concerns with mobile payments. What security aspect are you most concerned with?

Percent, except as noted	
Q40	
Hackers gaining access to my phone remotely	45.6
Someone intercepting my payment information or other data	32.8
Losing my phone or having my phone stolen	16.6
Malware or viruses being installed on my phone	2.7
Other	1.7
Refused to answer	0.6
Number of respondents	**745**

Table B.41. Assuming that the reason(s) you do not currently use mobile payments was addressed, which of the following activities would you be interested in performing with your mobile phone?

Percent, except as noted	
Q41	
Making payments directly to another person	17.1
Waving or tapping my mobile phone at the cash register to pay for a purchase	17.2
Paying bills online	34.4
Transferring money to friends or family in another country	7
Using your mobile phone as a "virtual wallet" to replace all the cards you currently carry in your wallet	16.6
Buying goods or services online	21.9
Receiving/using coupons on your phone	27.7
Receiving specials and discount offers based on your location	21.6
Other payment-related activities	12
Refused to answer	15.2
Number of respondents	**1,780**

Table B.42. Please rate the security of SMS (text messaging)

Percent, except as noted	
Q42	
Very safe	8.3
Somewhat safe	30.1
Somewhat unsafe	16.4
Very unsafe	10.8
Don't know	33.1
Refused to answer	1.2
Number of respondents	**2,002**

Table B.43. Please rate the security of mobile browsers similar to the way you access the Internet on your PC

Percent, except as noted	
Q43	
Very safe	5.6
Somewhat safe	36
Somewhat unsafe	18.8
Very unsafe	7.6

Percent, except as noted	
Q43	
Don't know	30.2
Refused to answer	2
Number of respondents	**2,002**

Table B.44. Please rate the security of an application downloaded from your phone's mobile app store

Percent, except as noted	
Q44	
Very safe	7.4
Somewhat safe	32.9
Somewhat unsafe	15.1
Very unsafe	6.8
Don't know	36.1
Refused to answer	1.8
Number of respondents	**2,002**

Table B.45. How would you currently rate the overall security of mobile banking for protection?

Percent, except as noted	
Q45	
Very safe	5.1
Somewhat safe	27.8
Somewhat unsafe	20.7
Very unsafe	11.2
Don't know	33.9
Refused to answer	1.4
Number of respondents	**2,002**

Table B.46. Would you like to use your mobile phone for any of the following purposes, assuming they were made available to you?

Percent, except as noted	
Q46	
Buy things at the point of sale	25.2
Track your finances on a daily basis	31.1
Organize and track gift cards, loyalty and reward points	21.4
Compare prices when shopping	47.9

Table B.46. (Continued)

Percent, except as noted	
Q46	
As a ticket for buses, trains, or subways	18.7
As a key to enter your house	18.4
Purchase tickets to events	22.9
As a membership card (e.g., museums, gym, etc.)	24.2
To receive and manage discount offers and coupons	30.5
To receive offers and promotions based on where you are	33
As a form of photo identification	23.4
Refused to answer	18
Number of respondents	**2,002**

Table B.47. Banks can offer a service whereby checks to be deposited are photographed using your camera phone and the image is sent over the mobile Internet during a mobile banking session so that the bank can deposit the funds into your account without you having to present the physical check. The bank then sends a notification acknowledging receipt of the deposit. If your bank offered this service, how likely would you be to use it?

Percent, except as noted	
Q47	
I already use it	3.9
Very likely	13.7
Somewhat likely	24.1
Somewhat unlikely	20.8
Very unlikely	36.4
Refused to answer	1.1
Number of respondents	**2,002**

Table B.48. Before going to a retail store to make a large purchase, do you generally compare prices online?

Percent, except as noted	
Q48	
Yes	58.4
No	41.1
Refused to answer	0.4
Number of respondents	**2,189**

Table B.49. Before going to a retail store to make a large purchase, do you generally look at product reviews online?

Percent, except as noted	
Q49	
Yes	57.6
No	41.6
Refused to answer	0.7
Number of respondents	**2,189**

Table B.50. Online shopping is when you go to a merchant's website through your web browser or an application and make a purchase. Have you ever used your mobile phone for online shopping?

Percent, except as noted	
Q50	
Yes	16.4
No	82.3
Refused to answer	1.4
Number of respondents	**2,002**

Table B.51. Have you ever used your mobile phone to comparison-shop over the Internet while at a retail store?

Percent, except as noted	
Q51	
Yes	19.4
No	79.4
Refused to answer	1.2
Number of respondents	**2,002**

Table B.52. Have you ever used a barcode scanning application on your mobile phone while shopping at a retail store to find the best price for an item?

Percent, except as noted	
Q52	
Yes	12.3
No	86.7

Table B.52. (Continued)

Percent, except as noted	
Q52	
Refused to answer	0.9
Number of respondents	**2,002**

Table B.53. Has using your mobile phone to compare prices while you were shopping at a retail store ever changed where you made your purchase?

Percent, except as noted	
Q53	
Yes	65.6
No	34.4
Number of respondents	**393**

Table B.54. Have you ever used your mobile phone to browse product reviews while shopping at a retail store?

Percent, except as noted	
Q54	
Yes	16
No	83.2
Refused to answer	0.7
Number of respondents	**2,002**

Table B.55. Has reading product reviews on your mobile phone while shopping at a retail store ever changed which item you ended up purchasing?

Percent, except as noted	
Q55	
Yes	76.9
No	22.5
Refused to answer	0.6
Number of respondents	**289**

Table B.56. In the past 12 months, have you used your mobile phone to check your account balance or available credit before making a large purchase?

Percent, except as noted	
Q56	
Yes	67.2
No	32.1
Refused to answer	0.7
Number of respondents	**372**

Table B.57. Thinking of the most recent time that you used your mobile phone to check your account balance or available credit before making a large purchase, did you decide not to buy that particular item because of the amount of money left in your account or the amount of your available credit?

Percent, except as noted	
Q57	
Yes	59.2
No	40.5
Refused to answer	0.3
Number of respondents	**242**

Table B.58. Have you signed up to receive coupons or special offers by e-mail from retail stores in the past 12 months?

Percent, except as noted	
Q58	
Yes	37.9
No	60.7
Refused to answer	1.4
Number of respondents	**2,290**

Table B.59. Have you made a purchase as a result of receiving one of these coupons or special offers?

Percent, except as noted	
Q59	
Yes	73.4

Table B.59. (Continued)

Percent, except as noted	
Q59	
No	25.8
Refused to answer	0.8
Number of respondents	**881**

Table B.60. Have you ever signed up to receive coupons/offers from a website such as Groupon or Living Social?

Percent, except as noted	
Q60	
Yes	28.2
No	70.5
Refused to answer	1.2
Number of respondents	**2,290**

Table B.61. Have you ever used a coupon from a website such as Groupon or Living Social?

Percent, except as noted	
Q61	
Yes	56.7
No	43.3
Number of respondents	**657**

Table B.62. New mobile contactless payments are becoming available from some banks, credit card companies, and transit operators. These let consumers tap or wave their mobile phone at a terminal instead of swiping a card. If you were offered the option of using this service, how likely would you be to use it?

Percent, except as noted	
Q62	
I already use it	1
Very likely	9.9
Somewhat likely	23.1
Somewhat unlikely	22.4
Very unlikely	42.3
Refused to answer	1.3
Number of respondents	**2,002**

Table B.63. How likely do you think it is that mobile contactless payments will become a major form of payment in the next five years?

Percent, except as noted	
Q63	
Very likely	16.7
Somewhat likely	33.3
Somewhat unlikely	15.5
Very unlikely	11.5
Don't know	21.8
Refused to answer	1.1
Number of respondents	**2,002**

Table B.64. How much responsibility do you have for maintaining the household budget and managing household income?

Percent, except as noted	
Q64	
None or almost none	11.6
Some	10.9
Shared equally with other household members	26.9
Most	13
All or almost all	36.3
Refused to answer	1.3
Number of respondents	**2,290**

Table B.65. How much responsibility do you have for paying monthly bills (e.g., rent or mortgage, utilities, cell phone)?

Percent, except as noted	
Q65	
None or almost none	15.2
Percent, except as noted	
Q65	
Some	11.5
Shared equally with other household members	18.9
Most	10.8
All or almost all	42.1
Refused to answer	1.6
Number of respondents	**2,290**

Table B.66. How much responsibility do you have for shopping for household goods and groceries?

Percent, except as noted	
Q66	
None or almost none	9.2
Some	16.3
Shared equally with other household members	24.8
Most	13.3
All or almost all	34.8
Refused to answer	1.7
Number of respondents	2,290

Table B.67. How much responsibility do you have for making decisions about savings and investments?

Percent, except as noted	
Q67	
None or almost none	12.1
Some	9.9
Shared equally with other household members	35.4
Most	11.7
All or almost all	30
Refused to answer	0.9
Number of respondents	**2,290**

Table B.68. Do you or anyone in your household use a program or website to track household finances (for example, Quicken, Mint.com, Excel, or a website provided by your bank)?

Percent, except as noted	
Q68	
Yes	21.3
No	78.1
Refused to answer	0.6
Number of respondents	**2,290**

Table B.69. How long have you been using this program or website to manage your household finances?

Percent, except as noted	
Q69	
Less than a year	15.6
One to two years	17.9
Three to five years	22.9
More than five years	42.7
Refused to answer	0.8
Number of respondents	**514**

Table B.70. In a typical month, how often do you or another household member use this program or website?

Percent, except as noted	
Q70	
0	3.3
1	12.6
2	10.4
3	7.1
4	11.5
5	6.3
6	2.9
7	0.6
8	3.1
10	6.5
12	1.8
14	0.4
15	4.8
20	6.4
21	0.1
24	0.2
25	5.8
26	0.5
27	0.2
30	7.7
31	0.2
35	0.5

Table B.70. (Continued)

Percent, except as noted	
Q70	
40	0.3
45	0.1
50	0.9
60	0.3
Refused to answer	5.4
Number of respondents	**514**

Table B.71. Do you use your mobile phone to track purchases and expenses?

Percent, except as noted	
Q71	
Yes	7.3
No	91.7
Refused to answer	1
Number of respondents	**2,002**

Table B.72. What method(s) do you use to track purchases and expenses on your mobile phone?

Percent, except as noted	
Q72	
A mobile application for expense tracking	38.3
A spreadsheet	10.1
Online (using the web browser to access a website)	47.6
Send text messages	12.1
Take notes in a notepad or word processor	21.1
Refused to answer	3.4
Number of respondents	115

Table B.73. In a typical month, how often do you use your mobile phone to track purchases and expenses?

Percent, except as noted	
Q73	
0	2.9
1	2.7

Percent, except as noted	
Q73	
2	16.6
3	10.4
4	5.4
5	15.4
6	0.8
7	0.3
8	0.5
10	5.8
12	0.4
13	0.1
14	0.4
15	8.8
20	7.5
25	2.8
30	4.2
40	2.1
50	0.3
123	0.2
Refused to answer	12.6
Number of respondents	**115**

Table B.74. You previously mentioned that you receive text alerts from your bank. What kind of text alerts do you receive?

Percent, except as noted	
Q74	
Low-balance alerts	66.4
Payment due alerts	31.7
Saving reminders	3.1
Fraud alerts	30.3
Other	18.2
Number of respondents	**111**

Table B.75. Thinking of the most recent low-balance alert you received by text message, which of the following actions did you take after receiving the alert?

Percent, except as noted	
Q75	
Transferred money into the account with the low balance	57.6

Table B.75. (Continued)

Percent, except as noted	
Q75	
Deposited money into the account with the low balance	16.2
Reduced my spending	41.1
None of the above	15.9
Number of respondents	**78**

Table B.76. Has receiving payment due alerts improved your ability to pay your bills on time?

Percent, except as noted	
Q76	
Yes, by a lot	37.4
Yes, by a little	40.4
No	22.2
Number of respondents	**41**

Table B.77. Imagine that the interest rate on your savings account was 1 percent per year and inflation was 2 percent per year. After one year, how much would you be able to buy with the money in this account?

Percent, except as noted	
Q77	
More than today	5.6
Exactly the same	20.9
Less than today	70.4
Refused to answer	3
Number of respondents	**2,290**

Table B.78. Considering a long time period (for example, 10 or 20 years), which asset normally gives the highest return?

Percent, except as noted	
Q78	
Savings accounts	15.3
U.S. Government bonds	25
Stocks	55.8
Refused to answer	3.9
Number of respondents	**2,290**

Table B.79. If an investor who only owns two stocks right now decides to instead spread their money among many different assets (i.e., more stocks, add bonds, add real estate), their risk of losing money on their entire portfolio will do what?

Percent, except as noted	
Q79	
Increase	21
Decrease	52.4
Stay the same	22.5
Refused to answer	4.1
Number of respondents	**2,290**

Table B.80. If you were to invest $1,000 in a stock mutual fund for a year, it would be possible to have less than $1,000 when you withdraw your money

Percent, except as noted	
Q80	
True	76
False	20.3
Refused to answer	3.6
Number of respondents	**2,290**

Table B.81. Suppose you owe $1,000 on a loan and the interest rate you are charged is 10 percent per year compounded annually.
If you didn't make any payments on this loan, at this interest rate, how many years would it take for the amount you owe to double?

Percent, except as noted	
Q81	
Less than two years	11.7
Between two and five years	23.8
Five to nine years	34.2
Ten years or more	25.8
Refused to answer	4.5
Number of respondents	**2,290**

Table B.82. Imagine that your car breaks down and requires $400 worth of repairs in order to drive again. Based on your current financial situation, how would you pay for this expense? If you would use more than one method to cover this expense, please select all that apply

Percent, except as noted	
Q82	
Put it on my credit card	36.4
With the money currently in my checking account	40.8
By taking money out of my savings	21.5
Using money from a bank loan, line of credit, or overdraft	3.4
By borrowing from a friend or family member	17.5
Using a payday loan or deposit advance	2.9
By pawning something	6
Other	5.7
Refused to answer	2.9
Number of respondents	**2,290**

Table B.83. Which of the following statements comes closest to describing the amount of financial risk that you are willing to take when you save or make investments?

Percent, except as noted	
Q83	
Take substantial financial risks expecting to earn substantial returns	3.3
Take above average financial risks expecting to earn above average returns	14.6
Take average financial risks expecting to earn average returns	36.9
Not willing to take any financial risks	42.5
Refused to answer	2.6
Number of respondents	**2,290**

Table B.84. Suppose that you are the only income earner in the family, and you have a good job guaranteed to give you your current income every year for life. You are given the opportunity to take a new and equally good job, with a 50–50 chance that it will double your income and a 50–50 chance that it will cut your income by one-third (33 percent). Would you take the new job?

Percent, except as noted	
Q84	
Yes	24.1
No	73

Percent, except as noted	
Q84	
Refused to answer	2.9
Number of respondents	**2,290**

Table B.85. Now suppose that the chances were 50–50 that it would double your income and 50–50 that it would cut your income by half (50 percent). Would you still take the new job?

Percent, except as noted	
Q85	
Yes	36.2
No	63.1
Refused to answer	0.7
Number of respondents	**547**

Table B.86. Now suppose that the chances were 50–50 that it would double your income and 50–50 that it would cut your income by one-fifth (20 percent). Would you now take the new job?

Percent, except as noted	
Q86	
Yes	22.5
No	76.8
Refused to answer	0.7
Number of respondents	**1,687**

Table B.87. Summary Statistics for Demographics

	Mean	**Standard Deviation**
Age	46.6209	16.9178
Male	0.4841	0.4999
Female	0.5159	0.4999
Ages 18–29	0.2139	0.4101
Ages 30–44	0.2599	0.4387
Ages 45–60	0.2755	0.4469
Ages over 60	0.2507	0.4335
Less than high school	0.1267	0.3327
High school degree	0.3035	0.4599
Some college	0.2875	0.4527
Bachelor's degree or higher	0.2822	0.4502

Table B.87. (Continued)

	Mean	Standard Deviation
White, non-Hispanic	0.6795	0.4668
Black, non-Hispanic	0.1158	0.3200
Other and two or more races, non-Hispanic	0.0679	0.2516
Hispanic	0.1369	0.3438
Less than $25,000	0.2154	0.4112
$25000–$39,999	0.1734	0.3787
$40,000–$74,999	0.2623	0.4400
$75,000–$99,999	0.1293	0.3356
Greater than $100,000	0.2195	0.4140
Married	0.5279	0.4993
Unmarried, widowed, divorced, or living with partner	0.4721	0.4993
Northeast	0.1842	0.3877
Midwest	0.2174	0.4126
South	0.3659	0.4818
West	0.2324	0.4225
Employed	0.5559	0.4970
Unemployed but in labor force	0.0970	0.2961
Not in labor force: retired, disability or other	0.3470	0.4761
Observations	2,290	

Table B.88. Use of online banking on a desktop, laptop, or tablet computer in the past 12 months by age

Percent, except as noted			
Age categories	Yes	No	Total
18–29	24.6	10.6	20.1
30–44	30.4	16.8	26
45–59	24.7	32.5	27.2
60+	20.3	40.1	26.7
Number of respondents	1,358	644	2,002

Table B.89. Use of mobile banking in the past 12 months by age

Percent, except as noted			
Age categories	Yes	No	Total
18–29	43.5	16.8	22.4
30–44	35.7	24.7	27
45–59	14.7	30.2	26.9
Percent, except as noted			

Age categories	Yes	No	Total
60+	6.1	28.4	23.7
Number of respondents	**372**	**1,626**	**1,998**

Table B.90. Use of mobile payments in the past 12 months by age

Percent, except as noted			
Age categories	**Yes**	**No**	**Total**
18–29	37.3	20.3	22.4
30–44	35.9	25.6	26.9
45–59	16.9	28.5	27
60+	10	25.7	23.7
Number of respondents	**213**	**1,780**	**1,993**

Table B.91. Use of online banking on a desktop, laptop, or tablet computer in the past 12 months by race

Percent, except as noted			
Race/ethnicity	**Yes**	**No**	**Total**
White, Non-Hispanic	73.3	68.8	71.8
Black, Non-Hispanic	7.6	13.4	9.4
Other, Non-Hispanic	5.7	4.8	5.4
Hispanic	12.4	12.2	12.3
2+ Races, Non-Hispanic	1.1	0.7	1
Number of respondents	**1,358**	**644**	**2,002**

Table B.92. Use of mobile banking in the past 12 months by race

Percent, except as noted			
Race/ethnicity	**Yes**	**No**	**Total**
White, Non-Hispanic	60.3	71.5	69.2
Black, Non-Hispanic	16.2	10	11.3
Other, Non-Hispanic	5.2	5.8	5.6
Hispanic	17.1	11.6	12.8
2+ Races, Non-Hispanic	1.2	1.1	1.2
Number of respondents	**372**	**1,626**	**1,998**

Table B.93. Use of mobile payments in the past 12 months by race

Percent, except as noted			
Race/ethnicity	Yes	No	Total
White, Non-Hispanic	58.3	70.8	69.3
Black, Non-Hispanic	12.9	10.9	11.2
Other, Non-Hispanic	7.1	5.4	5.6
Hispanic	20.9	11.6	12.8
2+ Races, Non-Hispanic	0.9	1.2	1.2
Number of respondents	**213**	**1,780**	**1,993**

Table B.94. Use of online banking on a desktop, laptop, or tablet computer in the past 12 months by gender

Percent, except as noted			
Gender	Yes	No	Total
Female	51.9	52.3	52.1
Male	48.1	47.7	47.9
Number of respondents	**1,358**	**644**	**2,002**

Table B.95. Use of mobile banking in the past 12 months by gender

Percent, except as noted			
Gender	Yes	No	Total
Female	53.4	52.9	53
Male	46.6	47.1	47
Number of respondents	**372**	**1,626**	**1,998**

Table B.96. Use of mobile payments in the past 12 months by gender

Percent, except as noted			
Gender	Yes	No	Total
Female	55	52.7	53
Male	45	47.3	47
Number of respondents	**213**	**1,780**	**1,993**

Table B.97. Use of online banking on a desktop, laptop, or tablet computer in the past 12 months by education group

Percent, except as noted			
Education	Yes	No	Total
Less than high school	5.2	16.7	8.9

Percent, except as noted			
Education	**Yes**	**No**	**Total**
High school	23.1	41.3	29
Some college	32.9	25.1	30.4
Bachelor's degree or higher	38.8	16.9	31.8
Number of respondents	**1,358**	**644**	**2,002**

**Table B.98. Use of mobile banking in the past 12 months
by education group**

Percent, except as noted			
Education	**Yes**	**No**	**Total**
Less than high school	5.5	12.1	10.7
High school	21.5	31.8	29.6
Some college	39	27.4	29.8
Bachelor's degree or higher	34	28.8	29.9
Number of respondents	**372**	**1,626**	**1,998**

**Table B.99. Use of mobile payments in the past 12 months
by education group**

Percent, except as noted			
Education	**Yes**	**No**	**Total**
Less than high school	7.2	11.2	10.7
High school	27.9	29.9	29.7
Some college	37	28.7	29.7
Bachelor's degree or higher	27.9	30.1	29.9
Number of respondents	**213**	**1,780**	**1,993**

**Table B.100. Use of online banking on a desktop, laptop, or tablet
computer in the past 12 months by income group**

Percent, except as noted			
Income group	**Yes**	**No**	**Total**
Less than $25,000	10.1	27.1	15.6
$25,000–$39,999	17.2	19.3	17.9
$40,000–$74,999	28.5	27.1	28.1
$75,000–$99,999	15.9	11	14.4
$100,000 or greater	28.2	15.5	24.2
Number of respondents	**1,358**	**644**	**2,002**

Table B.101. Use of mobile banking in the past 12 months by income group

Percent, except as noted			
Income group	**Yes**	**No**	**Total**
Less than $25,000	12.8	19.9	18.4
$25,000–$39,999	19	16.6	17.1
$40,000–$74,999	27.5	26.5	26.7
$75,000–$99,999	12.9	14	13.8
$100,000 or greater	27.9	22.9	24
Number of respondents	**372**	**1,626**	**1,998**

Table B.102. Use of mobile payments in the past 12 months by income group

Percent, except as noted			
Income group	**Yes**	**No**	**Total**
Less than $25,000	19.1	18.5	18.5
$25,000–$39,999	20.6	16.7	17.2
$40,000–$74,999	23	27.2	26.7
$75,000–$99,999	11.7	14	13.7
$100,000 or greater	25.6	23.6	23.9
Number of respondents	**213**	**1,780**	**1,993**

End Notes

[1] The Pew Research Center reports that 35 percent of American adults owned a smartphone as of May 2011. Pew Internet study, 2011, *35% of American Adults Own a Smartphone* (http://pewinternet.org/~/media//Files/Reports/2011/PIP_Smartphones.pdf).

[2] In its July 2011 report on smartphone banking security (based on a March 2011 survey), Javelin Strategy and Research finds that 19 percent of U.S. consumers are using mobile banking. Javelin, 2011, "Smartphone Banking Security: Mobile Banking Utilization Stalls on Consumer Fears."

[3] Javelin, 2011, *Smartphone Banking Security: Mobile Banking Utilization Stalls on Consumer Fears*.

[4] Federal Deposit Insurance Corporation, *2009 Survey of Unbanked and Underbanked Households* (www.fdic.gov/ householdsurvey/full_report.pdf).

[5] Pew Internet study, 2011, *35% of American Adults Own a Smartphone* (http://pewinternet.org/ ~/media//Files/Reports/ 2011/PIP_Smartphones.pdf).

[6] Ibid.

[7] Center for Financial Services Innovation (CFSI), 2010, *Financial First Encounters: An Examination of the Fractured Financial Landscape Facing Youth Today* (http://cfsinnovation.com/sites/ default/files/first_encounters_white_paper_12_16_0.pdf).

[8] There is a wide range of estimates of mobile banking adoption. comScore estimates that 13.9 percent of all mobile phone users had adopted mobile banking as of Q2 2011. Javelin estimated that 19 percent of mobile phone users had adopted mobile banking as of March 2011 (Smartphone Banking Security Report); however, the firm subsequently reports that mobile banking adoption jumped to 30 percent as of June 2011 (comScore, 2011, *Mobile Banking Financial Institution Scorecard*).

[9] The denominator for each of the questions on mobile banking adoption varies, thus the potential adoption rate is less than the sum of the percentages of respondents who indicate that they have or will adopt mobile banking. There are a total of 2,002 mobile phone users in our survey: 418 are current users of mobile banking, 182 report that they are likely to use mobile banking in the next 12 months, and 246 report that they will likely use mobile banking at some point in the future (for a total of 846 potential users, or 42 percent of all 2,002 mobile phone users).

[10] Bucks, Brian K., Arthur B. Kennickell, Traci L. Mach and Kevin B. Moore, 2009, "Changes in U.S. Family Finances from 2004 to 2007: Evidence from the Survey of Consumer Finances," *Federal Reserve Bulletin* (www.federalreserve.gov/ pubs/bulletin/2009/pdf/ scf09.pdf).

In: Mobile Financial Services
Editor: Silas Paulsen

ISBN: 978-1-62618-703-0
© 2013 Nova Science Publishers, Inc.

Chapter 3

STATEMENT OF KENNETH C. MONTGOMERY, FIRST VICE PRESIDENT AND CHIEF OPERATING OFFICER, FEDERAL RESERVE BANK OF BOSTON. HEARING ON "DEVELOPING THE FRAMEWORK FOR SAFE AND EFFICIENT MOBILE PAYMENTS"[*]

Chairman Johnson, Ranking Member Shelby, and members of the Committee, thank you for inviting me to appear before you today to talk about consumers' use of mobile financial services.

My testimony today will discuss development of the mobile payments system in the United States, and activities and progress of a mobile payments industry workgroup (MPIW) first convened by the Federal Reserve Banks of Boston (FRB Boston) and Atlanta in January 2010 to facilitate a discussion among key mobile industry stakeholders as to how a successful retail mobile payments ecosystem could evolve in the U.S. This group includes representatives of several large banks, credit card and automated clearing house (ACH) networks, the two largest mobile carriers, intermediaries/third-party payment processors, Internet payment service providers, mobile technology and security providers, handset and chip manufacturers, mobile and payment trade organizations, and a merchant trade group. Representatives from the Board of Governors of the Federal Reserve and United States

---

[*] This is an edited, reformatted and augmented version of the testimony given on March 29, 2012 before the Senate Committee on Banking, Housing, and Urban Affairs.

Treasury also participate. This workgroup has continued to meet three to four times each year since the initial 2010 meeting.

EVOLUTION OF MOBILE PAYMENTS AND BANKING IN THE U.S.

Before turning to mobile payments and banking, it may be helpful to provide brief context about the post-World War II history of the U.S. payments system. Looking back, banks and policymakers in the 1950s and 1960s were grappling with significant problems created by the growth of economic and financial activity relative to our ability to process paper payments and other financial instruments. At that time, retail payments were largely made by cash and checks. The use of computers to automate banking processes was just beginning. Since then, the U.S. payments landscape has changed dramatically. Electronic payments made through payment card networks and the automated clearing house system have become increasingly prevalent, and now represent about four out of every five noncash payments in this country. Virtually all check payments, which have been declining in number since the mid-1990s, are now cleared electronically, rather than in paper form. The cumulative effects of automation and innovation have driven several waves of new banking and payment services that continue to improve the efficiency and effectiveness of our payment systems.

The evolution of mobile banking and payments encompasses a combination of continued advances in hardware, software, and payment systems, including contactless payments, online banking, mobile phones (particularly smartphones), applications, and the convergence of Internet or e-commerce and mobile-commerce.

Since the late 1980s, companies and industries around the globe have experimented with different payment mechanisms aimed at improving access to banking services and the efficiency and ease of use for retail point-of-sale payments. For example, a contactless technology was developed in Japan, which a major commuter railroad in Tokyo implemented in a proprietary reloadable prepaid card. In addition to transit fare, consumers could use the contactless card to pay for purchases at merchants equipped with contactless readers near train stations. A similar product, also based on this contactless technology, was launched in Hong Kong's transit system in 1997. In the same year, a RFID[1] contactless payment system that allowed customers to wave/tap a fob to pay at the pump, was launched, the first of its kind in the U.S.

In the late 1990s, Finland launched a number of mobile commerce and banking initiatives. The first two mobile phone-enabled vending machines, which accepted payment via mobile phone text messaging, were installed in Helsinki. A bank in Finland launched the first mobile banking service to monitor account activity using this technology.

In the early 2000s, an online payment platform emerged that allowed consumers to email payments to each other. In 2002, online auctions were enabled to receive electronic payments from participants, replacing paper checks. Eventually, the online payment platform was expanded to online merchants.

U.S. consumers began to embrace online banking in the early 2000s. By October 2002, 34 million consumers, (representing 30 percent of U.S. Internet users) used online banking, an increase of 19 million consumers performing online banking since March 2000.

Initiatives that would allow consumers to use their mobile phones to perform new functions surged in 2000, driven by the development of mobile Internet access, the popularity of the Internet and e-commerce, and the increased awareness of mobile phones as more than voice communication tools. However, these service offerings did not meet consumer expectations and neither the phones nor the mobile networks handled data well, which led to very low adoption rates. The arrival of 3G[2] services in the mid-2000s addressed earlier technology problems and had a revolutionary impact on mobile technology in the U.S. Mobile phone manufacturers introduced smartphones that were enabled with more effective web browsing and data capabilities.

By 2006, helped by increased Internet and online banking adoption, and availability of smartphones, banks began to reexamine the development of mobile banking capabilities. Six of the largest ten U.S. banks offered mobile banking services by the end of 2007. Initially most banks offered browser and Short Message Service (SMS) based services, but in 2007, the mobile banking/payments market underwent a major transformation with the introduction of a new generation of smartphone. Now customers were able to download banking applications and other more advanced applications used for mobile-commerce that were not SMS-based, providing customization and improved security. The success and rapid growth of these and other smartphones led to increasing use of downloadable mobile applications for mobile banking and payments. By 2008, core deposit processors and mobile solution vendors began to develop software solutions tailored to financial institutions, enabling smaller U.S. banks to also offer mobile banking services.

Beginning in 2005, two payment networks launched several U.S. card and mobile contactless trials, which typically took place in metropolitan areas and ran for four to six months. The trials involved using a mobile phone to pay for in-store purchases at selected convenience stores and fast food restaurants, purchase transit tickets, or purchase concession items at sports venues. Although some trials proved the viability of Near Field Communication[3] (NFC) contactless technology, no full-scale deployments followed. In 2009-2010, several NFC initiatives were taking place in Turkey, Singapore, and the U.K., and NFC-enabled phones were introduced in Canada.

Several new mobile payment services were introduced within the last three years that could have a major impact on mobile payments in this country. In 2009, a new attachable card reader that plugs in to a smartphone was introduced, enabling small merchants to accept credit and debit cards. In 2011, a number of companies and industry partnerships announced mobile/digital wallet solutions utilizing NFC or cloud technology.

Mobile payments have been referred to as the "next payments revolution" by some industry participants. As mobile wallet technology, built upon the NFC contactless chip and secure element[4] for improved security and convenience, appeals to a broader array of consumers, and as merchants, banks, payments systems participants, and technology and telecommunications providers derive increased revenue or lower costs as a result of broad adoption, mobile payments should significantly change domestic and global payments practices.

WHY THE FEDERAL RESERVE SYSTEM CONVENED THE MPIW

The Federal Reserve strives to foster the safety and efficiency of the nation's payment systems. We monitor the evolution of retail payments through a variety of means, including a triennial Retail Payments Study[5] and an annual Survey of Consumer Payment Choice.[6] Of particular interest has been the migration of retail payments from traditional to emerging platforms, including the evolution of mobile banking and payments.

When FRB Boston began to research mobile banking and payments, our goal was to better understand how the industry was evolving, the factors that would motivate interaction and cooperation between mobile carriers and U.S. banks, the major barriers to adoption, and the impact of mobile payments on consumers in the U.S. payment system. We had seen mobile payments evolving more quickly in other parts of the world and wanted to understand why progress in the U.S. was slower. In late 2009, the large U.S. banks were developing mobile banking solutions, and regional and small banks were beginning to assess their business cases for mobile banking, but the concept of using a mobile phone to make a purchase was just surfacing.[7]

In conversations FRB Boston had with bankers and payments experts in 2009, we heard that they were concerned with fragmentation and lack of communication among key stakeholders, particularly mobile carriers, about the direction of mobile payments in the U.S. Industry participants suggested that the Federal Reserve facilitate a conversation among a diverse group of mobile payment stakeholders. Realizing that mobile payments would impact consumers in new ways, we wanted to ensure that all stakeholders adequately addressed issues related to consumer protection and security. Additionally, mobile carriers, which had limited understanding of banking and payment systems, would have an important role in the evolution of mobile payments, which introduced new coordination issues. Lastly, we believed that mobile payments, correctly implemented, could create new efficiencies in payments and possibly create new, cost effective, alternatives for the unbanked and the underbanked. As a result, the Federal Reserve hosted the first meeting of the MPIW in January 2010, to facilitate discussion on the evolution of mobile retail payments in the U.S.

OBJECTIVES OF THE MPIW

The overarching goal of the Federal Reserve in convening the MPIW was to encourage growth and innovation in the mobile payments market while minimizing risk to consumers and the payment system. The Federal Reserve believed it was important to gain an industry perspective to determine what barriers existed to the proper evolution of this market and whether we could help eliminate these barriers. We also wanted to explore how we might collaborate on issues of mutual interest. Thus, the objective for the first meeting was to have the experts inform and educate us, and to engage in an open cross-industry dialogue.

Many of the organizations represented at the meeting were already involved in mobile payment initiatives in Asia, Africa, and Europe. In the

U.S., a variety of very limited NFC contactless pilots were underway that enabled contactless payments initially on credit and debit cards and then mobile phones, but none with any lasting commercial availability. The industry was struggling to define a direction for mobile payments because of conflicting business models and strategies, and a lack of demonstrated consumer demand.

The main objectives for the group were to (1) gain a mutual understanding of the evolution of mobile retail payments in the U.S.; (2) provide a forum for participants to assess challenges, find points of mutual value, share ideas, and build consensus in a non-binding, free market manner; and (3) identify possible opportunities for future collaboration to help build critical mass for the success of mobile payments in the U.S.

WHAT THE MPIW HAS COMPLETED TO DATE

Recognizing the diversity of industries in the MPIW, subsequent meetings attempted to level set the group by covering each organization's initiatives relative to mobile payment plans, and perspectives on the benefits and barriers to implementation. Participants identified as benefits of mobile payments:

- The ability to reduce fraud using an encrypted contactless mobile platform.
- Potential merchant cost efficiencies gained by processing mobile payment transactions considered more secure than card transactions because of the use of dynamic data versus static magnetic card data, and reducing potential costs associated with PCI (Payment Card Industry) security standards compliance.
- Consumer convenience and value using a mobile wallet containing multiple payment methods stored securely in the mobile device, along with loyalty cards, virtual coupons, and discounts customized to reach different demographic cohorts determined by location- based, real-time capabilities of mobile technology.
- The ability to use a mobile phone to provide financial services to the unbanked and underbanked consumer segments.

Despite the benefits, participants identified a number of barriers that have impeded the growth of mobile payments, including:

- Lack of consumer demand, driven by the availability of many safe alternative payment choices in the U.S. and few differentiating factors or substantial benefits that consumers can see yet from mobile payments.
- Lack of NFC-enabled smart phones. This obstacle may be partially addressed as several handset manufacturers have committed to making more NFC-enabled phones in 2012.
- Lack of a standard business model (bank-centric, carrier-centric, partner or nonbank- centric), creating market fragmentation and limits mass adoption.
- Small percentage of merchant terminals that accept contactless NFC payments today. The capital investment in point-of-sale equipment for contactless technology is expensive, so merchants have been reluctant to make investments until they are certain of the direction in which the market is headed. They must now also factor in the implementation of EMV technology in the U.S., given the recent Visa/MasterCard mandate of compliance beginning in 2013.[8] However, this mandate may encourage faster implementation of NFC as part of the EMV implementation, or at least provide a deadline for compliance.
- Uncertain revenue models and lack of collaboration. Two NFC mobile wallet providers are aggressively seeking merchants to participate in their programs, and offering incentives for eligible consumers to use their mobile phones to pay for purchases. These commercial trials test new revenue models and partnerships to determine whether collaboration among stakeholders is successful.
- Participants also identified other barriers, such as the uncertainty regarding who owns the customer relationship (banks or mobile carriers), lack of global standards, and unclear regulatory direction as hindering the growth of the market.

Building on the identified benefits and challenges, the MPIW discussed the need for a roadmap to develop a high-level framework for the U.S. mobile ecosystem. This roadmap would include best practices and industry standards to manage the technology, security, settlement risk, and customer requirements at different points in the value chain. The MPIW also wanted to understand the roles of regulators for mobile payments and the applicable regulations. The MPIW then worked to define the principles essential to addressing the barriers and ensuring a successful mobile payment ecosystem in the U.S. Participants agreed in general with the principles related to mobile security, interoperability, and consumer protection, although there was not unanimous support on all details. These principles formed the basis of a white paper on the future of point-of-sale mobile payments in the U.S., *Mobile Payments in the United States Mapping out the Road Ahead,* published in March 2011.[9] Although written by the Federal Reserve, it reflected the general thoughts of the MPIW. These foundation principles are summarized below:

- Creation of an "open mobile wallet" that supports multiple payment options (credit, debit, bank account, prepaid/stored value, etc.) stored in a secure element in the phone, with broad payment and merchant marketing value options, such as rewards, coupons, and loyalty programs, enabling consumer choice.

- Use of NFC technology for contactless mobile payments at point-of-sale, along with enabling secure mobile applications. NFC must be based on industry standards, capable of supporting all payment methods and networks, and operable globally and in multiple venues (e.g. retail, transportation, ATM).

- Clearing and settling payments through existing channels (credit, debit, prepaid, ACH, mobile), but open to new channels. Existing payment mechanisms are the necessary foundation for the mobile payments platform to allow for mass adoption and consumer choice. New payment channels should be permitted but must be interoperable with the existing clearing/settlement system.

- Deployment of dynamic data authentication (DDA) as part of the security and fraud mitigation program for card-based mobile payment transactions. DDA generates a unique one-time cryptogram for each transaction, which is verified by interaction between the encrypted information on the chip and the network server when the transaction is authorized. Using contactless chip technology for mobile payments can reduce fraud because even if payment card information is stolen it cannot be used to make counterfeit cards or fraudulent online transactions.

- Development of mobile payment standards for the U.S. based on international standards and an industry-supported certification process to ensure domestic and global interoperability. The MPIW discussed potential gaps in standards for rules and best practices, and possible existing banking standards or rules that could be applicable to mobile phones with some modification. The payments business has well-defined groups that set standards, such as the American National Standards Institute and NACHA. Who would promote the adoption of the standards by the mobile payments industry is an open issue. Participants suggested that the U.S. consider working with existing mobile standards bodies, such as GSMA, GlobalPlatform, and NFC Forum, as appropriate, to identify gaps in coverage, and develop globally interoperable standards.

- Clarity of regulatory responsibilities among bank and nonbank regulators needs to be established early on, with input from the mobile stakeholders. While current regulations and rules may cover underlying payment methods, there is confusion because multiple regulatory agencies have responsibility for different aspects of payments and wireless transactions. Industry participants urged bank and nonbank regulators, such as the Federal Communications Commission, the Federal Trade Commission and the Consumer Financial Protection Bureau, to collaborate to define the regulatory environment for all the participants.

  For example, data privacy was a major concern. Complexities arise when different parties begin to share data. The potential marketing value of customer data when tied to mobile payments is significant. Data must be managed carefully to avoid potential abuse and unauthorized access to mobile payments data (e.g. transaction data, location-based data, etc.).

- Trusted Service Managers (TSMs) should manage and control the provision of secure elements in the mobile phone to control risk and ensure interoperability between mobile platforms. Although a broader role for the TSM was mentioned, the MPIW believed it was too early in the mobile payments evolution to consider this option.

Several major initiatives occurred after the paper was published in March 2011. First, the Federal Reserve and MPIW members began discussing the basic principles at payment industry conferences, and with payment trade groups, individual organizations, and regulators to collect feedback and escalate issues.

Second, to get input from a broader group of stakeholders, we invited several merchants, a prepaid card provider, debit card networks, a global mobile standards body, and consumer- focused organizations to the July 2011 MPIW meeting. The merchants raised several issues. They remain concerned about their business case – processing costs, investment in terminal upgrades, and cost of PCI compliance. Merchants would like to collect marketing data that will enable them to offer loyalty programs, customized coupons, and merchant rewards that provide consumers with a better shopping experience and increase sales. Because of the large capital investment, they would like to see a roadmap that clearly illustrates the industry direction for mobile payments, including mobile wallets.

Third, we created a sub-group to identify security pros and cons related to retail mobile payments that use contactless NFC (SIM, micro SD and embedded chip) or cloud technology. FRB Boston plans to publish a report of the findings later this year.

CURRENT STATUS OF THE U.S. MOBILE PAYMENTS LANDSCAPE

The volume of mobile Internet and remote purchases (m-commerce) is still small, but growing as the number of mobile applications increases, and more consumers own smart phones (about 45 percent adoption in the U.S. currently). As consumers have more opportunities to receive mobile coupons, discounts, rewards and location-based offers, the incentives to use mobile payments will further increase.

NFC contactless technology is being implemented in conjunction with several mobile wallet solutions at retail point-of-sale locations; however, alternatives to NFC do exist. QR codes[10] are in use at a few retailers for prepaid mobile purchases. Cloud technology, where payment credentials are stored on a secure file server that communicates with the merchant terminal for payment, rather than in a secure element on the physical mobile phone, is another emerging alternative. In the current mobile market, some of the large players continue to invest in NFC, others are developing wallets in the cloud, and still others are covering all bases by providing mobile services for both NFC and cloud. It is feasible that these technologies will co- exist in the mobile payment ecosystem.

Nonbanks are substantially influencing the evolution to mobile payments. In 2011, several commercial partnerships and joint ventures were announced for retail mobile wallet payments. Additionally, an online payment platform announced plans to enable brick-and-mortar merchants to accept payments from its wallet accounts.

The initial offering uses a mobile phone number, not a mobile phone. Several new entrants to the payment system are enabling small merchants to accept card payments using their mobile phones with a plug-in device and a mobile application, while others serve as intermediaries to handle payments for digital content billed directly to mobile carriers.

Some smartphones are being used for functions previously performed on personal computers.

These devices became a game changer because they provided consumers with an interface to the web and many new applications. Consumers demonstrated their desire to use their smartphones for multiple functions, which led to even more new applications. The smartphone helped to build consumer experience and prepare the environment for mobile payments.

NEXT STEPS

The Federal Reserve will continue to facilitate the dialogue among MPIW participants and other stakeholders and monitor progress in the evolution of mobile payments. The next MPIW meeting is scheduled for April 2012. This meeting, which will include bank and nonbank regulatory agencies, will focus on issues related to security, privacy, and consumer protection, and respective oversight responsibilities.

Future MPIW efforts will focus on education that is needed to help consumers understand steps they can take to protect their mobile financial data, including using passwords to lock their devices to prevent access to sensitive data, mitigation tools that allow for remote device deactivation and wiping of data, and alerts of suspicious activity.

The Federal Reserve will continue to conduct research to better understand consumer needs, behaviors, and adoption plans related to mobile payments. In addition, the Federal Reserve plans to work with industry participants to identify potential gaps in security and fraud prevention, and potential mitigation strategies for the different mobile payment technologies (NFC versions and cloud).

We plan to encourage the mobile stakeholders to work together to define the respective responsibilities of the various parties (e.g., the phone, mobile carriers, processors, banks, and settlement systems) to ensure robust end-to-end security, and to develop security rules and standards for eliminating or appropriately mitigating risks for mobile payments.

CONCLUSION

Collaboration among mobile industry stakeholders, the Federal Reserve, and interested government agencies through the MPIW has helped to educate diverse participants on different views and concerns around mobile payments, and awareness of the need for collaboration in certain areas, such as security and standards. Going forward, the MPIW will continue to provide a forum to discuss issues and barriers as they arise with an objective of more timely resolution. The MPIW enables proprietary innovation to occur, while promoting a shared framework for interoperability. Finally, working with mobile carriers, banking and payments industry participants, and government regulators, the Federal Reserve hopes to help mobile payments in the United States evolve in an efficient and safe manner and provide a convenient payment option to all consumer segments.

Thank you again for inviting me to appear today. I am happy to answer any of the committee's questions.

End Notes

[1] RFID or Radio Frequency Identification Device is a tag or transponder used to identify and transmit data short distances in one direction via radio waves.

[2] 3G (generation) mobile services provided more bandwidth for faster Internet access from a mobile phone, as well as advanced media features.

[3] Near Field Communication or NFC is a short-range wireless proximity technology that uses radio frequency to enable two-way communication between devices. NFC chips are embedded in mobile phones to enable contactless 'tap and go' payments.

[4] Combination of hardware, software, interfaces and protocols that enable secure storage and use of credentials for payment, authentication and other services

[5] http://www.frbservices.org/communications/payment_system_research.html

[6] http://www.bos.frb.org/economic/ppdp/2011/ppdp1101.htm

[7] Banks had shown significant interest in the previous three years, but many preferred to be fast followers, not leaders. Most banks, except the very large, were moving slowly, waiting for others to demonstrate the viability of mobile payments. Only 1,000 of the approximately 17,000 banks offered mobile banking in the U.S. at the end of 2009. However, 40 percent of U.S. consumers used online banking. Many stakeholders believed that in 2010 and 2011 there would be significant momentum leading the financial services industry to become more involved in mobile (banking and payment) services. They noted, however, that many smaller U.S. banks and credit unions look to their existing third-party core deposit processors to deliver solutions without significant upfront cost.

Contactless cards, introduced several years ago in the U.S., were not successful and did little to generate demand for mobile payments. Poor marketing and education may have contributed. Many cardholders received contactless cards but were unaware that they had them or how to use them and did not know whether merchants they frequented accepted contactless payments.

[8] EMV is a global standard for credit and debit payment cards based on chip card technology, taking its name from the card schemes Europay, MasterCard, and Visa, which developed it. The standard covers the processing of credit and debit card payments using a card that contains a microprocessor chip at a merchant payment terminal. The transactions are referred to as "chip and PIN" because PIN entry is usually required to verify the customer is the genuine cardholder. The EMV standard has been implemented in most developed countries, other than the U.S. In August 2011, Visa announced a phased EMV migration plan for the U.S. In January 2012, MasterCard announced its own EMV adoption program. Both programs incorporate similar incentives and timelines designed to encourage migration by processors and acquirers by April 2013, and retailers by mid-2015 (2017 for automated fuel dispensers).

[9] http://www.bos.frb.org/bankinfo/firo/publications/bankingpaypers/2011/mobile-payments-mapping.htm

[10] For mobile payments, QR codes are two-dimensional barcodes that can be read by smartphones with a mobile application to pay for purchases or receive mobile coupons.

In: Mobile Financial Services
Editor: Silas Paulsen

ISBN: 978-1-62618-703-0
© 2013 Nova Science Publishers, Inc.

Chapter 4

STATEMENT OF MICHAEL L. KATZ, SARIN CHAIR IN STRATEGY AND LEADERSHIP, UNIVERSITY OF CALIFORNIA, BERKELEY. HEARING ON "DEVELOPING THE FRAMEWORK FOR SAFE AND EFFICIENT MOBILE PAYMENTS, PART 2"*

Chairman Johnson, Ranking Member Shelby, and members of the Committee, thank you for inviting me to appear before you today to talk about mobile payments.

America's consumers are increasingly connected via smart phones, tablet computers, and other mobile devices. Many people have predicted that the use of near-field communications (or NFC), a technology which allows consumers to pay by swiping their phones rather than their credit or debit cards, will revolutionize consumer payments at bricks- and-mortar merchants. I disagree. I believe the changes associated with NFC and so-called digital wallets will be evolutionary, not revolutionary. There *will* be a revolution resulting from the ubiquity of smart phones and tablets, but that revolution will manifest itself in the ways merchants manage their relationships with their customers.

Today, merchants and consumers already have access to a wide range of payment options, including cash, checks, and various payment cards. These options are easy to use, widely accepted, and trusted. Moreover, most

---

* This is an edited, reformatted and augmented version of the testimony given on July 10, 2012 before the Senate Committee on Banking, Housing, and Urban Affairs.

consumers already have established relationships with payment service providers, and merchants have made significant investments in equipment, systems, and employee training to utilize these payment services. In order for new payment services based on smart phones and tablets to compete successfully, these services will have to offer merchants and consumers additional value in comparison with current options. Cool technology alone will not be enough.

Merchants will be attracted to mobile payments if those services either lower the merchants' costs of completing transactions or attract additional consumer patronage. How will mobile payment services attract customers to bricks-and-mortar merchants? Surveys demonstrate that consumers want payment services that are widely accepted, easy to use, and trustworthy. So how do mobile payments stack up against the competition?

When it comes to paying at bricks-and-mortar merchants, the extent of acceptance is a weakness, rather than strength. Indeed, mobile payment services face a chicken-and-egg problem. Specifically, a merchant does not want to bear the expense of changing its checkout process to accommodate a new payment service if there are few consumers who use that service. Similarly, a consumer does not want to sign up for the payment service if there are few merchants who accept it. But if everyone waits for everyone else to join first, the new service will never get off of the ground. There are several potential solutions to the chicken- and-egg problem but all of them rely on a common underlying factor: there has to be some source of benefit that makes it worthwhile to invest in overcoming the chicken-and-egg problem. So we are back to looking for the source of consumer value.

An NFC-enabled digital wallet can be more convenient and possibly easier to use than a conventional wallet filled with multiple payment cards. It is worth observing, however, that most of us are going to have to carry conventional wallets anyway, at least until drivers' licenses and insurance cards and the like also go digital. Moreover, is it really that much easier to swipe your phone than a smart card? In the short run, ease-of-use benefits appear to be too limited to be a significant driver of adoption.

That leaves trust as a source of value. Security and privacy are two critical elements of trust. Consumer surveys reveal that many consumers question the security of mobile payments, and indeed mobile payment systems do have points of vulnerability, such as the radio interface, that card-based systems do not. Moreover, through the use of malicious code downloaded through apps or web browsing, a smart phone can be compromised without the attacker's having to attain physical proximity. Consequently, security is not going to be a positive driver of mobile payment adoption any time soon. Things do not look more promising in terms of privacy. Consumer surveys reveal that many consumers worry that mobile payment companies will collect too much personal information and that that information will be misused.

If ubiquity, ease of use, and trust all create too little value to drive widespread adoption of mobile payments, what will? I believe the answer lies in the very information that consumers worry will be misused. The widespread adoption of smart phones and other mobile devices with increasing capabilities has made it possible to collect detailed data about where consumers are and what they are doing. This information can be analyzed to predict consumer behavior and used to generate personalized, context-specific, merchant-to-consumer communication delivered in real time. The ability to predict consumer behavior and send such targeted messages is a very powerful marketing tool that will be worth tens of billions of dollars annually to merchants.

A hypothetical example illustrates some of the possibilities. A mobile payment app might alert a coffee retailer at 10:45 a.m. that a person who on most days purchases a cup of coffee by 10:30 is just leaving her office and has yet to visit a coffee shop today. Taking into account the summer heat and the fact that the retailer is not very crowded right now, the retailer could send an email or text message to the consumer offering a 20-percent discount on an iced coffee if she comes into the store three blocks away in the next 30 minutes. In summary, information and communication lie at the heart of the coming mobile payment revolution.

Mobile payments represent the convergence of three industries: telecommunications, banking, and web services. This industry convergence is going to lead to complex regulatory convergence as well. The interplay of economy-wide antitrust policy and privacy regulation with the sector-specific regulatory regimes for banking and telecommunications is going to be problematical for the industry. It may also confuse consumers and given them false senses of security and/or risk. However, properly implemented, regulation could foster well-placed consumer trust and, thus, promote the adoption of mobile payments. Given the importance of information and the complexity of the issues involved in regulating the collection and handling of it, public-policy concerns regarding privacy will loom large for years to come.

Thank you again for inviting me to appear before you today. I would be happy to answer any questions you might have.

In: Mobile Financial Services
Editor: Silas Paulsen

ISBN: 978-1-62618-703-0
© 2013 Nova Science Publishers, Inc.

Chapter 5

STATEMENT OF THOMAS P. BROWN, ADJUNCT PROFESSOR, BERKELEY LAW SCHOOL, UNIVERSITY OF CALIFORNIA. HEARING ON "DEVELOPING THE FRAMEWORK FOR SAFE AND EFFICIENT MOBILE PAYMENTS, PART 2"[*]

Chairman Johnson, Ranking Member Shelby, and members of the Committee, thank you for inviting me to appear before you today to discuss mobile payments.[1]

Historically, innovation in the payment industry has not been a subject of public interest. I attribute this relative disinterest to the fact that recent innovation in the payment industry has been invisible to consumers. For more than a quarter of a century, the basic mechanics of engaging in a payment transaction have not changed even for payment cards, the newest of our payment technologies: approach point of sale, select card from wallet or purse, hand card to cashier (or swipe the card yourself), and wait for a message that the transaction has been authorized (or declined). Although industry participants can rightly claim that they have radically transformed the process of authorizing the transaction in the past three decades, most consumers don't see it this way.[2]

---

[*] This is an edited, reformatted and augmented version of the testimony given on July 10, 2012 before the Senate Committee on Banking, Housing, and Urban Affairs.

The phrase "mobile payments" elicits a different reaction. People are genuinely excited about mobile payments. Some of this excitement stems from the eye-popping valuations that some providers of mobile payments have reported to the technology press. But much of it appears to flow from anticipation that the mash-up of mobile with payments will bring a bit of magic to the point of sale. Waving a phone just seems cooler than swiping a plastic card.

Although I look forward to the day when I no longer have to carry plastic or paper to buy things, we should not, in my view, measure the success of mobile payments by the speed with which waving replaces swiping. Existing payment technologies work very well in traditional retail environments. In fact, one might say that they were made for each other. The retail environments that Americans experience most often—multi-lane retailers, gas stations, quick- service restaurants—were designed to take full advantage of the virtues of existing payment mechanisms (primarily speed at the point of sale). And mobile payment technologies will not soon displace the well entrenched incumbents.

With that said, the bundle of technologies that we generally label "mobile" is rapidly transforming the payment industry. Mobile devices are being turned into Point Of Sale ("POS") systems. This is enabling millions of new merchants to accept electronic payments. It is also rapidly changing how existing merchants engage their customers inside and outside of traditional retail environments. These changes hint at the potentially radical ways in which mobile payments will change how people shop, buy, sell and pay for goods and services. It is possible— though not certain—that mobile payments will further undermine the distinctions between financial services companies, retailers and communications providers. But these really are just hints. At this point, it is impossible to say with any real confidence how mobile payments will affect banks, payment companies, merchants and customers. It is also far too early to pick winners (or losers) among the many mobile payment technologies and companies now emerging.

In my view, lawmakers should be wary of claims that mobile payments need to be further regulated, particularly in the areas of information security and privacy. The payment industry, including the mobile payment piece, is already heavily regulated. New layers of regulation could easily stifle innovation and benefit some providers at the expense of others. And any new laws or regulations directed at the burgeoning mobile payment industry should be developed on the basis of a concrete understanding of the laws and regulations now in place.

With that preface, I will describe the existing regulatory framework for the payment industry, discuss what's truly new about mobile payments, and address potential issues related to consumer privacy and compatibility.

EXISTING REGULATORY FRAMEWORK

Participants in the mobile payments space already face substantial costs associated with complying with the existing regulatory regime. Firms that want to enter the business typically confront a choice between obtaining licenses on a state-by-state basis or working under the regulatory authority of a chartered financial institution. And once that threshold is crossed, firms in the payment industry shoulder a long list of compliance obligations.

Generally speaking, a firm that wants to enter the payment business faces a stark choice: find a suitable regulated chartered partner (*i.e.* a bank or other depository institution) or obtain licenses from all 50 states as a money services provider. The first option brings the mobile payments provider under the indirect supervision of the state and federal agencies responsible for regulating the chartered partner (*e.g.* FDIC or OCC). This option also carries costs associated with revenue-sharing and compliance, although some compliance costs and responsibilities may be shared with the chartered partner. The second option brings the mobile payments provider under the direct supervision of various state entities. It also brings with it the initial burden of acquiring state licenses—potentially a multi-year process with associated fees and costs that can easily exceed a million dollars. Annual maintenance costs for state licensing can also be significant.

Beyond this choice, firms in the payment industry must comply with a long list of laws and regulations. Regulation of consumer financial services is complicated. Payments companies—mobile payments included—are typically bound by federal law providing consumers with recourse in the event of a disputed charge.[3] Firms that rely on a stored value purse to support their payment applications may be required to implement Customer Identification Programs and to report suspicious transactions to the federal Financial Crimes Enforcement Network (FinCEN).[4] Firms that support international payments must scrutinize their operations for compliance with the requirements laid down by the Office of Foreign Assets Control (OFAC). Firms that store customer bank account or other payment account data are also subject to state laws governing notification to customers and state entities when that personal information is compromised.[5] Finally, although the full scope is still being fleshed out, the Consumer Financial Protection Bureau has supervisory authority over certain "covered persons," including nonbanks.[6]

One potential way to reduce costs is to eliminate the requirement that an entity must be licensed by all 50 states to operate nationally. There is no apparent benefit, from a prudential standpoint, of such a fragmented regulatory regime. This is not to say that licensing itself has no value—as in the banking industry, some supervision likely helps ensure that mobile payment companies can meet their obligations to consumers. This value becomes diluted, however, when that mobile payments company must contend with the overlapping, but not identical, regulatory requirements across the 50 states. In other contexts, state-regulated entities are able to "passport" a single state license across all 50 states, so that compliance with that individual state's regulations suffices to allow those entities to do business nationwide.[7]

POTENTIAL BENEFIT: THE MOBILE POINT OF SALE

Although most of the conversation surrounding mobile payments focuses on the possibility of using mobile phones instead of plastic cards to initiate transactions, mobile's initial impact on the payment industry has been felt on the receiving side of the transaction. Existing forms of payment are mobile at least from the perspective of the consumer (*i.e.*, with rare exceptions, our wallets and purses follow us wherever we go). Until recently, however, electronic payment systems were limited to environments that could be reached by fixed line communication systems. Advances on the mobile front are releasing this constraint.

The transformation of mobile devices into Point Of Sale ("POS") systems is taking place on a number of fronts:

- Mobile devices have enabled millions of informal merchants to accept electronic payments. With an app and a small (generally free) device that plugs into the mobile device (known as a "dongle"), artisans, contractors and farmers now accept payment cards from their customers instead of cash.
- Mobile devices are changing how people shop. By equipping sales associates with tablets and smart phones and sending those associates onto the store floor, traditional retailers are turning the entire retail environment into the point of sale. Customers can make purchases in the aisle, rather than waiting to pass through the check-out line.

- Some retailers are using their customers' mobile devices to extend the point of sale outside the store. They are allowing customers to use their mobile devices to make purchases on their mobile phones (and tablets), go to the store, take the item off the shelf, and walk out of the store without ever having to present a payment card to a sales associate.
- Mobile devices are rapidly changing how people purchase information goods like books, music, movies and software. Again, the mobile device is the point of sale. Consumers use their own tablets and smart phones to access digital marketplaces, purchase books, songs, apps, etc., and read, listen to and use those goods.

The transformation of the consumer's mobile device into a primary point of contact between the merchant and the consumer may have a dramatic effect on retail commerce. People tend not to share their mobile devices in the same way that they share laptops and personal computers. This creates the opportunity for merchants to create customized offers for consumers. Most offers currently take the form of discounts, location based offers and fairly basic extensions of traditional loyalty programs (*e.g.*, buy nine coffee drinks and get the tenth free).

This evolution in payment technology may make it possible for restaurants and other small retailers to employ some of the dynamic pricing techniques that have been reserved to large-scale travel businesses. Outside of the travel industry, customers in most retail environments confront a single set of prices. Although different customers may be willing to pay very different prices for essentially the same service, it is difficult for traditional retailers to distinguish one customer from another. As merchants use mobile payment technologies to engage more directly with their customers, they may begin to employ some of the same strategies used by airlines, hotels and car rental companies to maximize traffic in their stores and restaurants, setting lower prices for some customers and higher prices for others. The extension of dynamic pricing strategies from the nation's airlines to the corner store may not be universally hailed.

MOBILE PAYMENTS AND PRIVACY

In order to customize experiences for particular customers, the merchant (or payment provider) must have access to information about those customers.

For example, imagine a restaurant owner trying to craft an offer to attract new customers to her restaurant. Our hypothetical restaurant owner would likely want to reach out to those customers whose spending habits indicate that they like to eat out but who have never eaten at her restaurant. But the restaurateur would likely want to limit the offer to customers who live in the local area, excluding from the scope of the offer tourists and people traveling though the area on businesses. Such distinctions immediately implicate concerns about consumer privacy.

The legal and regulatory framework that governs the collection and use of information regarding consumers is complex and fragmented. Regulatory requirements vary by industry. Financial institutions and affiliated third parties, for example, face one set of requirements under the Gramm-Leach-Bliley Act.[8] Credit reporting companies face another set of requirements under the Fair Credit Reporting Act.[9] Health care providers face another set of requirements under the Health Insurance Portability and Accountability Act's ("HIPAA") Privacy Rule.[10] Federal law also imposes specific restrictions on the sharing of information about certain kinds of purchases.[11] Special rules apply to certain kinds of information, and the rules can vary depending on the manner in which the information is held at the time of disclosure.

Communications in transit receive a different set of protections, for example, than information at rest.[12]

No single agency is responsible for administering federal privacy law. The FTC has shown the most consistent interest in the subject, though the Department of Justice gets involved, too, particularly when a third party obtains information by illegal means. The prudential agencies have historically been responsible for ensuring that the financial institutions that fall within their purview adhere to the requirements of Gramm-Leach-Bliley. Dodd-Frank has further complicated this picture by severing responsibility for supervising adherence with GLB's privacy requirements from responsibility for supervising adherence to its information security and disposal requirements.[13]

State laws add another level of complexity. A number of states purport to limit the information that can be collected from consumers in connection with certain types of transactions. California law, for example, forbids merchants from, as a condition of sale, requiring or requesting personal identification information from consumers who use a credit card at a point of sale,[14] and the California Supreme Court has defined a zip code to be personal identification information.[15] And, as noted above, forty-six states have enacted laws requiring that consumers receive notice if certain information is obtained by a third party.

Private law also plays an important role in this area. The major card networks restrict the uses to which transaction data can be put. Visa's Operating Regulations prohibit a merchant from disclosing a cardholder account number, personal information, or other Visa Transaction Information to any entity other than a registered third party agent, the acquirer, or the acquirer's agent, and that such disclosure must be made for the sole purpose of (i) assisting the merchant in completing the initial merchant transaction, or (ii) as specifically required by law. The payment card networks, through the PCI Council, also regulate how merchants and other participants in the payment card systems may store information related to payment card transactions.

This complex suite of laws does not advance a single policy objective. Much of federal privacy law is based on the principle that consumers should receive notice and choice with respect to the use of information about them when that information is being used for marketing purposes. As some commentators have observed, it is far from clear that consumers actually want to receive such notices.[16] Other aspects of federal privacy law are directed at protecting consumers against misuse of data that relates to them. The Do Not Call Registry and the liability caps for unauthorized transactions under Regulation Z and Regulation E fall into this category.[17] Moreover, to the extent that privacy laws attempt to enable consumers to shield their identities from mobile payment providers or other financial institutions, they work at cross purposes with federal banking law, which as noted above requires firms to collect enough information about their customers to report suspicious transactions.

This complexity should lead lawmakers and regulators to take particular care before creating new laws under the privacy banner. Most efforts to protect consumer privacy interests simply make it more costly for firms to collect information from consumers and to share that information with other firms. But information sharing is not a concern *per se*, and the focus on sharing tends to distract attention from the problems that give rise to the concern about sharing in the first place—the misuse of sensitive information and the failure to take care against the exposure of sensitive information to malicious third-parties.

COMPATIBILITY

This leaves the question of compatibility. Of the issues on today's agenda, this is the most complex and nuanced.

Compatibility (or incompatibility) issues can arise at many different levels. My iPhone is not, for example, compatible with my aunt's Android device. My phone has a different operating system from hers, and it connects to one telecommunication network—Verizon— while hers connects with another—AT&T. My device supports some applications that hers does not. In this sense they are incompatible. But in another sense, they are deeply compatible. Even though the phones are different in many ways, I can use my phone to call or send emails and texts to hers. If we both have accounts with PayPal or Dwolla, I can use my phone to send her money.

As mobile technologies grow in importance as platforms for the exchange of value, compatibility issues are likely to arise. Every mobile payment application may not work in every environment. Starbucks, for example, may choose to keep its mobile payment application separate from that offered by Peet's. But incompatibility issues at that level should not be a source of concern. Indeed, the decision to offer a closed loop payment product may reflect regulatory distinctions as much as anything.[18]

With that said, concerns about the interoperability of different mobile payment applications cannot be dismissed entirely. Both the telecommunications industry and the payment industry have borne witness to significant battles over network access and compatibility.[19] And those issues may surface again. Antitrust authorities in Europe are currently reviewing a proposed payment joint venture in the UK in part due to such concerns.

But—and this is a perspective informed as much by my background as an antitrust lawyer as a student of the payment industry—these issues are sufficiently nuanced that they are not susceptible to a one-size-fits-all solution. Issues of compatibility and interoperability need to be evaluated on a case-by-case basis. Firms may, as in the Starbucks example above, have good reason for rendering their payment applications incompatible with the applications offered by others. But they may not, and in some instances, incompatibility can be a cause for public concern. Fortunately, antitrust law provides a well-developed framework for analyzing these issues as they arise on a case-by-case basis.

CONCLUSION

This is an exciting time for the payment industry. Emerging technologies are creating opportunities for financial institutions, merchants and consumers to reinvent commerce. This innovation is taking place against the backdrop of a very complex regulatory regime, and although it is possible to imagine ways in which the regulatory burdens facing firms in the area could be reduced (particularly in the area of state-by-state licensing requirements), this emerging industry does not appear to need any new regulation.

Thank you again for inviting me to appear today. I am happy to answer any of the committee's questions.

End Notes

[1] I am appearing today in my capacity as an adjunct professor at Berkeley Law School. In my private practice, I have represented and currently represent a number of clients that participate in the mobile payments industry. The opinions expressed in today's testimony are my own and may not represent those of my firm or my clients.

[2] *See* Thomas P. Brown, *Keeping Electronic Money Valuable: The Future of Payments and the Role of Public Authorities, in* MOVING MONEY: THE FUTURE OF CONSUMER PAYMENTS 127, 132-33 (Robert E. Litan and Martin Neil Baily eds., 2009).

[3] For example, for mobile payment transactions involving credit cards, Regulation Z, which implements the federal Truth in Lending Act, limits a cardholder's liability to $50 for unauthorized charges. 12 C.F.R. pt. 226.12(c). Likewise, the federal Electronic Fund Transfer Act provides similar limitations on liability for unauthorized debit card charges. 15 U.S.C. § 1693g(a).

[4] All federally regulated banks are required to have a written CIP pursuant to section 326 of the USA PATRIOT Act.

[5] At this time, forty-six states, the District of Columbia, Puerto Rico, and the Virgin Islands have enacted such statutes. The National Conference of State Legislatures publishes a comprehensive list, *available at* http://www.ncsl.org/issues-research/telecom/security-breach-notification- laws.aspx.

[6] *See* 12 U.S.C. § 5514(a)(1)(C).

[7] For example, under the federal Secure and Fair Enforcement for Mortgage Licensing Act ("SAFE Act"), 12 U.S.C. § 5100 *et seq.*, mortgage loan operators enjoy uniform licensing standards nationwide, either through their home states' participation in the Nationwide Mortgage Licensing System and Registry or by those states' establishing individual systems that comply with certain federal standards.

[8] 15 U.S.C. § 6801 *et seq.*

[9] 15 U.S.C. § 1681 *et seq.*

[10] *See* HIPAA Privacy Regulations, 45 C.F.R. pt.160.

[11] For example, information regarding video or video game rental or sale records is protected from disclosure pursuant to the Video Privacy Protection Act, 18 U.S.C. § 2710.

[12] "Electronic communications," meaning any transfer of information through electronic means, are generally protected from disclosure under the federal Electronic Communications Privacy Act ("ECPA"), 18 U.S.C. § 2510 *et seq.* Title I of the ECPA, known as the Wiretap Act, protects electronic communications while in transit. Title II of the ECPA, known as the Stored Communications Act, protects communications held in electronic storage.

[13] The Dodd-Frank Act amended Title V of the Gramm-Leach-Bliley Act to grant rule-making authority under Sections 502-509 of that Act to the Consumer Financial Protection Bureau (CFPB).

[14] Cal. Civ. Code. § 1747.08(a)(1)-(2).

[15] *Pineda v. Williams-Sonoma Stores, Inc.*, 51 Cal. 4th 524 (2011).

[16] *See, e.g.*, J. Howard Beales, III & Timothy J. Muris, *Choice or Consequences: Protecting Privacy in Commercial Information*, 75 U. CHI. L. REV. 109, 113 (2008) ("Few consumers actually take the time to read [GLB notices], understand them, and make a conscious choice about whether to opt out of information sharing that is not a matter of statutory right for the financial institution.").

[17] *See id.* at 118-20 (explaining that the Do Not Call list addressed the problem of unwanted calls at home by focusing on the consequence—the call—rather than access to the information necessary to produce the call—the consumer's phone number).

[18] *See, e.g.*, 31 C.F.R. pt. 1022 (FinCEN's final rule relating to prepaid access).

[19] *See, e.g.*, *MCI Commc'ns Corp. v. Am. Tel. & Tel.*, 708 F.2d 1081 (7th Cir. 1983); *United States v. Visa U.S.A., Inc.*, 344 F.3d 229 (2d Cir. 2003).

In: Mobile Financial Services
Editor: Silas Paulsen

ISBN: 978-1-62618-703-0
© 2013 Nova Science Publishers, Inc.

Chapter 6

STATEMENT OF SARAH JANE HUGHES, MAURER SCHOOL OF LAW, INDIANA UNIVERSITY. HEARING ON "DEVELOPING THE FRAMEWORK FOR SAFE AND EFFICIENT MOBILE PAYMENTS, PART 2"[*][†]

Mr. Chairman, Ranking Member Shelby, and honorable members of the Committee, I am pleased to be invited to discuss mobile payments generally, and the benefits and risks that mobile payments offer to merchants and other users in the marketplace.

Mobile payments are among the most innovative payments options emerging across the world. They enable person-to-person and person-to-business payments using flip phones and text messaging (SMS) in less developed countries. In the developed states, where banking systems and telecom networks are more regulated, mobile payments are emerging as a handy means of making small-dollar payments in the person-to-person and person-to-business markets. Perhaps even more importantly in the United States, they are enabling the unbanked and under-banked to make payments at lower risk and cost than some of the other payment options they may have.

---

[*] This is an edited, reformatted and augmented version of the testimony given on July 10, 2012 before the Senate Committee on Banking, Housing, and Urban Affairs.

[†] My prepared remarks and any remarks I may make in response to your questions reflect only my own views and do not necessarily reflect the views of the Trustees of Indiana University or the Maurer School of Law.

Sponsors of mobile payments services vary significantly in size, the breadth and scale of the services offered, and the extent of federal or state regulation to which their businesses generally, and their payments services in particular, are subjected. Supervision and enforcement also differ significantly.

Mobile payments providers and developers of special mobile payments applications are attracting significant sums in capital investments, which suggest promising business models.

Nationwide merchants such as Starbucks were early adopters of mobile payments options for their businesses. Paying for a coffee or a snack could be completed before the foam on a specialty drink disappeared. Speedier payments, however, can be associated with business decisions to lower security safeguards – at least in the credit and debit industries.

Other merchants in the United States – including plumbers and participants in farm markets and craft shows, and increasingly non-profit organizations – are beginning to use mobile payments to take payments from their retail customers. These may be small transactions for a pound of field tomatoes, medium-sized transactions for the plumber's house call, or larger payments such as recurring utility, car finance or mortgage payments. But, unlike Starbucks where larger-dollar purchases are probably rare, non-profit organizations can take contributions or sell quantities of tickets that are much larger in dollar terms using mobile payments options. Small-dollar and larger-dollar transactions may present different risks for merchants, consumers, mobile payments providers, and the financial institutions that hold the funds sent or received via mobile payments.

So far, we have not heard much about larger-dollar payments being made for recurring purposes, such as mortgage payments or car finance installments, but there is little to stop that from happening from a technical or legal perspective. For these types of payments, banks have expressed concerns about the security of underlying banking account information in the hands of relatively new entrants to the payments industry.[1]

Your letter of invitation laid out many possible topics for witnesses to cover. I will focus my remarks on benefits and costs to merchants who take or might take mobile payments, and also to the other regulatory and enforcement issues their participation in payments may present. In some cases, the different issues that consumers and merchants have in the marketplace for mobile payments may converge; on others, they may diverge. I have identified five areas in which mobile payments are likely to benefit our economy and why they are so attractive to merchants, and five areas in which mobile payments present new concerns that may need to be regulated or harmonized and otherwise may require new enforcement approaches. In creating these lists, I made no assumptions about how regulation will evolve.

Turning first to potential benefits of mobile payments, I have five topics to cover and have provided one or more examples to illustrate the range of issues that may arise.

1.   Taking mobile payments is quick and functional.

Mobile payments – whether utilizing existing credit or debit card interchange services or "rails" or the services of telecom or other providers – have the potential to help the owners of small businesses, small non-profit organizations, and farmers and artisans who bring their goods to farmers' markets and craft shows collect payments from their retail customers.

Mobile payments are speedy: they take only a few seconds to process. They operate without expensive and bulky equipment. They do not require a heavy specialty card reader. (The "reader" for Square, for example, is only about an inch square and the connector fits into the plug on the seller's smart phone or tablet.) Small merchants using smart phone apps also can take checks from their retail customers, using a feature called "remote deposit." No doubt, members of the Committee have seen ads from USAA and other financial institutions for remote deposits for the service members, veterans, and their dependents and families who USAA serves.

In addition, mobile payments, as replacements for magnetic-stripe credit and debit cards, may enable merchants in the United States to skip the impending transition from mag-stripe to chip-and-pin cards and the new readers that chip-and-pin technologies require. Mobile readers may be less expensive than chip-and-pin systems.

2.   Taking mobile payments helps small business owners collect smaller sums due from retail customers and may help to expand the economy.

Two of the leading mobile payments services providers, Square and Intuit, count among their merchant customers thousands of small business operators (such as plumbers) and non-profit organizations (who take mobile payments for tickets sales and for contributions from supporters). The less time these merchants have to spend at tellers' windows or in line for the ATM, the more time they have to help customers, fixing leaking showers or providing services to the community. Thus, mobile payments may help smaller businesses maximize their productivity and add to the economy's health.

Mobile payments also help merchants at farmers' markets and craft fares make sales they otherwise might not – if the consumer involved has to stop and find an ATM machine before completing the purchase.

3. Taking mobile payments may help merchants deter fraudulent charges at the point of sale.

At two conferences in which I participated earlier this year, speakers explained in great detail why mobile payments were safer for consumers than payments with traditional plastic credit and debit cards; they paid less attention to whether they would be safer for merchants as well.

Unlike a tangible plastic credit or debit card whose credentialing and verification protocols – the account number, expiration date, customer name, and security code printed on the card itself – remains constant, mobile payments offer a more dynamic set of credentials that includes the mobile device's location at the time of the payment transaction and the ability of the mobile device to generate a unique identifier for every payment transaction. Dynamic credentialing is one feature that will help merchants – and consumers – avoid fraudulent charges.

Some mobile payments providers such as Square offer merchants another credentialing device – a real-time opportunity to match the face of the person offering to make the mobile payment with the face shown on the mobile device, or with the same merchant's record of the face of the person who last used the same mobile device to make a payment. Some consumers won't want merchants to store their photos for later purposes, but many probably won't care.

In addition, the geo-location of using the mobile device for "proximity" payments adds a security layer. Geo-location gives merchants – as well as processors and providers – an extra level of confidence that the mobile device from which the payment instruction or order is emanating is in fact the proper one.[2]

Dynamic credentialing, including facial recognition possibilities and geo-locational information, offers potentially greater safety in payments than the more static tangible plastic cards on which we have relied for the past 35 years or more.

The full-scale dynamic credentialing I have described – without going into detail about the technologies that support it, primarily because they are proprietary technologies in part – may not apply as functionally if the mobile device is being used to make a payment outside of the merchant's own store. Thus, "remote" mobile payments could raise some of the same fraudulent charge issues that merchants currently face in "card-not-present" transactions today in the credit and debit card payment spheres.

We do know that the card industry has created a payment application data security standard ("PA DSS"), much like its relatively successful PCI DSS set of security standards (for payment cards). But PCI DSS is not an ironclad solution to fraud risks from data interception or otherwise, as we learned from the episodes that TJX, Hannaford Brothers, and Global Payments experienced. Each of those companies had been PCI DSS compliant, but none were the nanosecond following the security breaches they suffered. And, once a retailer or processor falls out of compliance, it must re-prove its security procedures to qualify again.

4. **Taking mobile payments offers merchants opportunities to build customer loyalty through mobile-based rewards programs, geo-locationally based or individually directed advertising, and other information about customers derived from the payment transaction that can be re-used.**

In contrast to traditional tangible plastic credit and debit cards that carry only basic credentialing and payment information, mobile payments offer merchants potential means of communicating with customers that can help merchants build customer loyalty and promote special offers.

5. **Taking mobile payments allows merchants to reach consumers who do not have demand deposit accounts or their equivalents or credit cards.**

With estimates of the number of unbanked adults in the United States upwards of 30 million households [check most recent figure – FTC or FRB March, 2012], merchants who take mobile payments may get customers who otherwise would have to pay in cash.[3]

Unbanked consumers, particularly recent immigrants, often have smart phones instead of traditional computers and use smart phones – via mobile payments and mobile banking – to make payments to retailers and creditors.

Unbanked persons' adoption of mobile payments adoption is a means of reducing their dependence on cash and cash equivalents such as money orders, and may serve as the basis for reducing their costs of participating in the retail economy and reducing the risks associated with carrying cash.

Now turning to possible risks or costs merchants (and consumers) may experience when taking mobile payments, we will see some overlap between risks present in credit and debit card transactions and risks in mobile payments.

New risks also may arise.

6. **Taking mobile payments may not be free from interception risks or from malware applied to the data streams along the path maintained by app providers, intermediary processors, and the ultimate payor (such as the financial institution or telecom) that have affected the credit card industry, and thus may pose security risks similar or additional to those in the current payments marketplace.**

Mobile payments providers emphasize the greater security at the point of sale that mobile payments can provide over credit or debit cards, for the reasons I have mentioned above.

What is less discussed is a possibility, if not a probability, that because the payments data and accompanying transaction data potentially move through more hands on their path to the ultimate payor, there is a greater likelihood of data interception (through war-driving interception as the data move from the mobile device to the merchant, and from the mobile device to a processor and then to the payor and then to the merchant – depending on the manner in which the payment is processed) or through malware introduced along the path.

More simply put, the more participants in payments processing the greater the number of opportunities for interception or the application of malware.

7. **Taking mobile payments and harvesting more consumer information from these payments transactions places more personally identifiable information in the hands of merchants and the payments system participants downstream from merchants – and imposes on them more extensive, and possibly different data-protection responsibilities than they formerly may have had.**

Among the counter-weights to the benefits merchants may gain from having more information about their customers and targeted, inexpensive means of communication with them about merchants' offers, merchants will find compliance responsibilities they may not have anticipated. The more participants in the mobile payments processing path, the greater the number of potential harvesters and holders of personally identifiable information and purchase histories.

The value of these data harvests features at least as prominently as the shares of available direct income from marketing the software and processing the payments is likely to offer – at least in the United States where payments processing had been become increasingly efficient (as with checks) or already has been regulated by Congress (debit card interchange and some credit card fee limitations).

Some of these participants are not familiar with federal and state privacy protections or with requirements of Gramm-Leach-Bliley's Title V (Privacy) and the federal Safeguards Rule, of the Fair Credit Reporting Act and the federal Disposal Rule, or with the Children's Online Privacy Protection Act ("COPPA")[4] and the COPPA Rule.[5] Some participants will not be covered by either of the first two Acts or rules, but probably are already covered by COPPA and its rule. Having suitable supervision from federal and state regulators and suitable enforcement resources to protect individuals and this nascent industry from bad publicity is an important goal.

The State of New Jersey recently entered into a settlement with a mobile app creator whose target audience was children.[6] The action, brought in the United States District Court for the District of New Jersey, alleged that 24 × 7 Digital, LLC, and its owners Mark Yamashita and Rei Yoshioka, "collected, maintained, and transmitted to a third party, personal information about children" in violation of COPPA and the COPPA Rule. Among the elements of relief to which the defendants agreed was the destruction of the children's personal information – including the information they transmitted – within five days of the entry of the order.

An additional issue with data collected, stored, and transmitted involves its treatment in a future bankruptcy proceeding of the collector, storage operator, and recipients. The Committee may recall the public furor over the fate of children's data in the early days of internet commerce involving an online children's toy store and a company called DoubleClick, and the tussle over whether the children's personal information – as part of the debtor's "customer lists" was eligible to be auctioned for the benefit of the debtor's general creditors.

8. Taking mobile payments does not necessarily relieve merchants of problems with charge-backs for fraudulent charges or other costs associated with data security problems.

As the Clearing House Association recently explained to the House Committee on Financial Services' Subcommittee on Financial Institutions and Consumer Credit, banks "are usually required to absorb fraud liability and always absorb the cost of re- credentialing [the consumer] regardless of whether they had any connection with the underlying breach that compromised the data."[7]

Another aspect of this issue is that merchants will be dealing with more players in the payment than they may be accustomed to, and this broader array of counter-parties means more contracts to negotiate and monitor. Contracts will assign settlement times, charge back rules, transactional limits, and costs. Providers may reserve the right to change the terms of these agreements frequently, and may or may not tolerate patterns of behavior that are less than fully compliant with the contracts' provisions. Merchants lose eligibility to participate (as happens upon occasion in the credit and debit payments industries) and have little ability to be restored to participation in their new-found payments tools.

9. Taking mobile payments does not relieve merchants of responsibility for payment data integrity or for post-payment data security, and, because of the growing number of payments systems participants, may increase time needed to explain payments to customers, increase fraud risks, and also may create new risks for institutions that hold funds and facilitate settlements.

This heading subsumes two subgroups of issues. The first relates to payment data integrity. Merchants need tools to prevent interference with the data stream so that a payment of $10 remains a payment of $10 as it moves through processing.

The second relates to post-payment data security at merchant's own locations and in their databases. Merchants need to safeguard data while the payment is being processed and for whatever time needed to respond to charge-backs, etc. They also need to dispose of the data properly and safely after it is not needed for any particular purpose or ultimately not needed to comply with applicable records retention requirements imposed by federal or state governments.

Data integrity (safeguards against alteration or replication of the sums the consumer intended to pay and the merchant wanted to receive) is important is all payments transactions. We have relatively elaborate rules for checks, credit and debit cards, and funds transfers (wholesale and retail) to protect data integrity and resolve disputes. For consumer transactions with credit and debit cards, federal law provides error resolution and liability limits.

We also want to provide for post-payment data security. Will the same standards that apply to storage of credit card information post-transaction/payment apply to mobile payments? Will merchants be required to store personally identifiable information related to the purchase separately from the payment transaction information? Will all intermediaries who can collect and maintain data be subject to the same obligations – whether from federal or state laws?

10. **Taking mobile payments may – but may not – require merchants to adjust their compliance with federal statutes, regulations, and executive orders pertaining to the deterrence of money laundering or prohibitions against doing business with concerns from designated foreign states or with "specially designated nationals" – individuals who are connected or suspected of being connected with drug or arms trafficking or support of terrorism– for purposes of compliance with the panoply of laws and executive orders enforced by the Department of the Treasury's Office of Foreign Assets Control.**

I have left for last the law enforcement issues on my list. Mobile payments offer a new set of opportunities to money launderers and those who would fund terrorists. Their person-to-person payments capacities and their speed and ease of transport are factors. Their abilities to dis-intermediate payments or to layer payments through multiple sets of hands are significant enticements for money launderers. Of these issues, speedy processing/settlements and disintermediation are the most problematic.

These laws are notoriously hard to enforce and preparing compliance plans for businesses eager to comply is a huge industry for law firms and consulting companies. Merchants hate these compliance responsibilities for their complexity and the effort required to train their rotating staffs.

Payments disintermediation generally, and perhaps the more so for mobile payments, is likely to make it harder for federal agents and local law enforcement to spot problems in local markets. Disintermediation in mobile payments also may hinder enforcement of AML and terrorist-finance control laws and agreements domestically and globally.

Sellers who take mobile payments also may have compliance responsibilities – as will providers and processors – with state safety and soundness registration and examination regimes for money services businesses and with state privacy and data security breach laws.

In closing, I have focused my remarks on domestic transactions and payments in which merchants in the United States and consumers here participate. Cross-border transactions and the payments associated with them raise other issues – issues that add significant dimensions to certain of the issues I have mentioned, with issues pertaining to charge-backs and error-resolution rules at one end of the spectrum, network and device compatibility in the middle, and issues pertaining to taxation and deterrence and identification of money laundering or terrorist support – given the wide array of providers and the technologies or business models they may deploy – at the opposite end.

Banks and consumers are justifiably concerned about broader access to customers' account information and the enticements that these data present to hackers, and even petty thieves. Consumers are justifiably nervous about the security of any personal information they convey to merchants through mobile devices and their geo-locational tracking properties. Consumers are justifiably concerned about who will have access to their personal information and payment account information as it travels, perhaps especially about how much third-party (and government) access there will be to it.

In terms of the future of regulation of mobile payments, we may see self-regulation, the existing mix of state and federal regulation and enforcement – or even some regional compacts such as those that spear-headed interstate banking in the 1980's, additional federal regulation or enforcement, or even a cross-border or multi-national regulation and enforcement scheme. A first task is to determine whether the different silos of providers – banks and other financial institutions (as defined by various federal laws), telecom providers, mobile app developers, and payments intermediaries who are in none of those industries – should be regulated under a common set of expectations and requirements, or should be regulated according to the role they play in mobile payments.

Thank you again for the opportunity to be with you today.

End Notes

[1] Statement for the Record from Robert C. Hunter, Deputy General Counsel, The Clearing House Association, L.L.C. to The Subcommittee on Financial Institutions and Consumer Credit of the House Committee on Financial Services, June 29, 2012 [hereinafter "The Clearing House Association, June 29, 2012 Letter"].

[2] The degree to which counterfeiting of mobile payments technology becomes an issue is yet unknown.

[3] Not having to handle cash or checks is a benefit to merchants all of itself in terms of accounting and fraud losses and speeds merchants' ability to get the proceeds of transactions into their bank accounts and forward to suppliers, landlords, and other creditors.

[4] 15 U.S.C. § 6501-6506 (2010).

[5] 16 C.F.R. Part 312 (2010).

[6] Chiesa v. 24 x 7 Digital, LLC, et al., Civ. No. 2:12-cv-03402 (Jun. 26, 2012) (consent decree and order for injunction and other relief).

[7] The Clearing House Association, Letter of June 29, 2012, supra note 2, at 1, 2, 5.

In: Mobile Financial Services   ISBN: 978-1-62618-703-0
Editor: Silas Paulsen   © 2013 Nova Science Publishers, Inc.

Chapter 7

TESTIMONY OF TROY LEACH, CHIEF TECHNOLOGY OFFICER, PCI SECURITY STANDARDS COUNCIL. HEARING ON "THE FUTURE OF MONEY: HOW MOBILE PAYMENTS COULD CHANGE FINANCIAL SERVICES"*

INTRODUCTION

Chairman Capito, Ranking Member Maloney, members of the Subcommittee, thank you for the opportunity to testify on the important issue of mobile payment security.

My name is Troy Leach and I am the chief technology officer of the PCI (Payment Card Industry) Security Standards Council. The Council is a global industry standards body focused on securing payment card data that is processed, stored, or transmitted regardless of the form factor, device or channel used to initiate payment. Formed in 2006 by the payment card brands American Express, Discover Financial Services, JCB International, MasterCard Worldwide and Visa Inc. to guide the development of open industry standards for global payment security, the Council has an active base

---

* This is an edited, reformatted and augmented version of the testimony given on March 22, 2012 before the House Committee on Finanical Services, Subcommittee on Financial Institutions and Consumer Credit.

of more than 600 global participating organizations representing leading industry players from the around the world.

As the payments environment changes, new technologies are introduced which must be evaluated to determine what new threats may also emerge. It is increasingly important to have a strong framework, driven by cross-industry collaboration to secure payment transactions to contain and reduce fraud for consumers and businesses globally.

Mobile technology offers many opportunities to grow consumer payments and also presents many challenges to secure sensitive payment information. As with any technology being considered for use in a payments environment, the Council's goal is to foster standards that help to minimize this risk to cardholder data. To this end, we have taken a leadership role by actively engaging with industry and other standards groups to proactively address the security of mobile payment acceptance. The Council's work is ongoing, and we have made significant progress.

My testimony today will outline the Council's focus on securing cardholder data, specifically in environments where mobile devices are being used as a new type of payment acceptance tool, and how we're applying our expertise to address the fast-paced evolution and adoption of mobile technology in the payments space. Currently, we are not addressing consumer-facing mobile payment technologies or solutions.

ABOUT THE PCI SECURITY STANDARDS COUNCIL

The Council's Mission

The Council was formed in 2006 by global payment card brands to work with industry stakeholders in guiding the development of open industry standards for global payment security.

Very simply, this means that the Council's goal is to foster standards to protect not just consumers, but also industry players such as merchants (retailers, transportation companies, hotels, etc), banks, government, academia and all other organizations that store, process and transmit cardholder data. It's this wide range of stakeholders that make up the Council's global base of more than 600 leading national, regional and global participating organizations.

The Council's Work

The growth and improvement in payment card security over the past 5 years has everything to do with global industry involvement in the work of the Council.

It's through the voluntary and active participation of this global community that the Council sets and develops technical standards and other resources that comprise the essential tools needed help to protect cardholder data against breaches and reduce payment card fraud. Protecting payment card data is a shared responsibility across the payments ecosystem. Together with our industry participants we drive education and awareness of payment security globally.

Today global adoption of the Council's standards and industry participation in the Council's process for standards development are at an all-time high. As a result of our collective efforts, we are seeing fewer large-scale card data breaches in the marketplace.[1] And when breaches do occur, organizations that have applied the Council's PCI Security Standards are in a better position to mitigate the impact of the compromise.[2] Together these industry standards provide the best baseline available for protecting payment card data. Indeed, other sensitive industries are modeling their own security standards on those developed by the Council.

THE COUNCIL'S ROLE IN MOBILE PAYMENTS

Our Focus

The Council's focus is the protection of cardholder data through implementation of its standards. Absent such safeguards, that data can be too easily accessed, and then used to commit fraud. It's through this lens that we evaluate mobile payments technology.

When discussing mobile payment security, it's important to differentiate between two different environments for the use of mobile devices:

1) Merchant acceptance applications where phones, tablets and other mobile devices are used by merchants as point-of-sale terminals in place of traditional hardware terminals, and

2) Consumer facing applications where the phone is used in place of a traditional payment card by a consumer to initiate payment. Several

standards groups have been involved and have focused on securing different parts of the mobile payments ecosystem with the aim to protect payment data.

The Council's security efforts to date in this area have been concentrated on work related to securing the use of mobile devices as a point of sale acceptance tool.

In line with the Council's focus on working with stakeholders to secure the entire payment card transaction– from point of entry of payment data to how it's processed through secure payment applications - the Council's efforts in the mobile area are centered around the impact of mobile payment solutions on merchant acceptance and processing channels.

Specifically, the Council is focused on mitigating the risk of mobile devices used to take payments from being tampered with; addressing the security of applications running on mobile devices that include or require card data; and the integrity of third-party services.

In the midst of an evolving payments landscape and threat environment, maintaining the security of cardholder data remains critical and an ongoing challenge. To address this fast-changing technology and continue to drive payment security forward, the payments industry needs to look to advancements in secure payment technology (e.g., through encryption) to reduce these risks by minimizing the value and exposure of cardholder data, and develop strong effective security practices and controls for mobile payments.

The payments industry must take a nimble and proactive approach, while continually evolving our strategies for risk management to adapt quickly to these ongoing changes.

As an open, global cross-industry organization focused on providing baseline standards for stakeholders to increase the security of payment transactions, the Council is well positioned to spearhead this effort. We recognize that payment security is a shared responsibility and requires active involvement from participants across the payment chain.

The Council is currently working with stakeholders from all sectors of the emerging mobile payment acceptance environment to collectively and effectively develop the standards and other tools necessary to help secure cardholder data in this manner.

Challenges and Risks

The ability to use mobile technology to accept and process payments undoubtedly offers great potential to the marketplace. However, the rapid innovation and complexity of the environment, present a number of challenges, including managing potential risks to payment information. In the midst of growing deployment of mobile technologies in payments, worries over security may potentially be a barrier to adoption.

While technologies that promise real solutions for securing mobile acceptance are quickly evolving, a number of security risks remain. These include: rapid and potentially insecure development of mobile applications; lack of traditional security controls such as effective software patch management and monitoring; potentially unauthorized access or too wide-spread privileges of third parties to access financial applications; and to the potential for the abuse protective measures such as data encryption or administrative controls. A failure to adequately address any of these valid concerns can put payment card data at risk.

Our Approach

The Council is applying its expertise to examine these risks within the context of the existing industry security framework that its PCI Security Standards provide – one that's built around the fundamental element of trust essential to enable mobile commerce to flourish.

For mobile technology to be adopted in the same way that traditional forms of payment are accepted, consumers and businesses alike need to be able to trust the ability of the technology to protect their payment data. It's also critical that they trust the service providers and other entities involved.

Trust is even more significant in the mobile payments environment because the environment is fragmented across manufacturers of devices, developers of Operating Systems, application designers, network carriers and the use of various protocols used to connect these different entities. Payment security is a shared responsibility. Ensuring mobile acceptance solutions are deployed securely requires that all parties in the payment chain work together in this effort.

To tackle this issue of trust the Council is working with a variety of stakeholders around the world. The goal is to identify and mitigate the risks that may arise when consumer and merchant roles converge to protect the device, the manufacturing of the device, the secure coding practices for software within those environments and the standards required to test and validate third-party entities that are involved in processing, storing and transmitting transaction data.

Securing Mobile Payments: Payment Acceptance Devices

Mobile phones have not traditionally been built to function as payment acceptance devices. Today, new capabilities are being added to these mobile devices to enable them to accept payment transactions. The integrity of the device that is being used to initiate a payment or access payment card-related information has to be trusted, and this trust must be based on real and robust security. Given this potential risk area to cardholder data, the integrity of the acceptance device is one of the Council's key focus areas in its work to address the mobile payment acceptance security.

The Council's existing standards include the PCI PIN Transaction Security (PTS) requirements[3] to provide security for physical devices accepting payments, such as point-of-sale terminals at the grocery checkout, gas pumps and airline ticket kiosks. The standard aims to ensure that the device is tamper-proof and if compromised, the data will be "zeroized", rendering it useless. At the end of 2011, the Council expanded the PTS requirements for protecting traditional swipe card terminals against tampering, to apply to mobile payment acceptance devices.[4]

The Council maintains a list on its website of approved devices that have been successfully tested in Council-approved laboratories to assist merchants in assessing the security of their currently deployed terminal devices, and in making informed future purchasing decisions.[5] This list is now expanding to include mobile, as well as traditional, acceptance devices.

Compliance by device vendors with the PCI PTS requirements allows merchants to use plug in devices with mobile phones to swipe cards securely by first encrypting the data at the point that the card is swiped to minimize risk by making it unreadable. The mobile device acts as a conduit and has no ability to decrypt the encrypted data.

Later this year, the Council plans to release specific guidance for merchants on how to effectively use these security requirements in conjunction with encryption technology to more easily and securely accept payments using mobile technology.

Securing Mobile Payments: Payment Software Applications

Today the entire shopping experience, from creating a grocery list to paying for the items on that list, can be realized using mobile technology. Retailers can get more customers through their store during a busy holiday season using payment software applications installed on a phone or tablet that transform these devices into a mobile cash register for quick and easy checkout. Consumers and businesses alike are benefiting from the convenience of mobile payments technology.

The potential for mobile technology to make things faster, easier and cheaper, both at home and in the workplace, domestically and around the world, means there is a growing market demand for businesses to use mobile applications to accept and process payments.

The security of software applications is one of the leading issues in securing mobile acceptance. Applications and acceptance devices must work together to realize a mobile payment transaction. Just as the integrity of the device has to be trusted, so does the integrity of the payment software application. As noted earlier, one of the key roles of the Council is not only to create the standards necessary to enable security, but also to educate the marketplace to the benefit of implementing these standards.

The PCI Payment Application Data Security Standard (PA-DSS) is the Council's standard for addressing the security of software applications.[6] It supports the Council's foundational standard for securing cardholder data, the PCI Data Security Standard (PCI DSS).[7]

Traditional payment applications range from touch screen applications you might see used in a restaurant, to point-of-sale software used in ticketing kiosks in museums and theme parks. Some of these payment applications may be designed to store cardholder data, putting this information at risk. Once again, the Council maintains a list of PA- DSS compliant applications. In this case, that list includes those applications that have been tested by Council-trained security assessors in laboratories and validated as secure. This list is available on the Council website for merchants to use in assessing their own applications and making informed purchasing decisions.[8]

It's against this standard that mobile payment acceptance applications are evaluated, recognizing that the strong technical requirements in this standard should be the baseline for any application accepting or processing payments – whether traditional or mobile.

As part of this evaluation, in 2011 the Council issued guidance on the types of mobile payment acceptance applications that can allow businesses to accept and process payments securely.[9] The Council published a checklist resource to help explain simply and succinctly to anyone currently considering mobile payment acceptance solutions which types of application support PCI Standards.[10] This resource, like all Council tools and resources, is available for download from the Council website free of charge.

The Council also identified the types of applications that fall short of security standards for secure mobile payment transactions. In collaboration with industry subject matters experts, including software application developers, the Council is continuing to examine this area to determine whether the inherent risk of card data exposure in these applications can be addressed by existing PCI requirements, or whether additional guidance or requirements must be developed.

Securing Mobile Payments: The Way Forward

The technology is here to make mobile payments a reality, and the possibilities are infinite. The Council's charter is to provide a forum for collaboration across the payments space to determine how the potential of mobile payment acceptance technology can be realized securely. The more pervasive mobile technology becomes the more we will see new threats and attack vectors that put data at risk. In tandem, other technologies for securing payments will emerge. It is, and for the future will certainly remain, a dynamic space.

As with all unchartered territory, trust must be established to make a way forward. In the case of mobile technology, this means establishing mechanisms and resources to build consumer and marketplace confidence that mobile payments are just as secure as credit or debit card payments. The Council will continue its consideration of extensions to its existing standards and the development of new standards to help ensure the trusted security of mobile payments and the devices that enable them. Additionally, this will mean working to enhance the security of entities across the payment chain who are involved in mobile acceptance, to ensure the existence of an industry standards framework to validate these entities, and to establish trust in the services these entities provide. This is an area that the Council will continue to examine moving forward.

In the meantime, great work is being done through the advancement of technologies in payments. The mobile phone will introduce new innovation but also may introduce new risks to payments. Our strategy for minimizing risk that can be added to a payment transaction by a mobile acceptance device is, where possible, to help eliminate card data from potentially insecure mobile environments. Technologies continue to emerge that offer the potential to both leverage the power of mobile computing and effectively reduce security risks by making payment data inaccessible or devaluing the data rendering it useless for committing fraud. The Council has already harnessed some of these technologies to address this dynamic environment and we will continue to assess and develop standards and guidance around them moving forward.

Payment security is a shared responsibility. The Council has engaged a wide range of industry participants in a collaborative effort to apply continued focus to the area of mobile payment acceptance security, including members across the mobile payments spectrum – from those who develop the applications and the phones themselves to those who are providing voice and data services. We are also working appropriately with other standards groups on this issue – such as EMVCo and BITS - and others across the board to address this multi-faceted challenge as an industry. Our outreach efforts to engage new players with whom we can work together to enable security in payments are ongoing.

The mobile payments environment, like other new and complex environments demands an understanding of many different perspectives. As a global industry group with members who represent the payment chain around the world, the Council is positioned to spearhead efforts to help ensure that payment security standards are addressing the mobile payments environment.

CONCLUSION

Once again, I want to thank Chairman Capito, Ranking Member Maloney, and the members of the Subcommittee for providing me the opportunity to testify on this important issue of mobile payment security. The PCI Security Standards Council's mission is securing payment data, including mobile acceptance. As the payments system changes and new technologies evolve, we will continue to work with our global stakeholders to develop the industry standards and provide the resources necessary for the protection of cardholder data across all payments channels and for the reduction of fraud for consumers and businesses globally.

End Notes

[1] Verizon Business 2011. "2011 Data Breach Investigations Report."

[2] The Ponemon Institute. 2011. "2011 PCI DSS Compliance Trends Study."

[3] PIN Transaction Security (PTS) requirements contain a single set of requirements for all personal identification number (PIN) terminals, including POS devices, encrypting PIN pads and unattended payment terminals. https://www.pcisecuritystandards.org/security_standards/documents.php?association=PTS

[4] PCI Security Standards Council. 2011. "PCI Council Updates PTS Program for PTS, Mobile." Press Release, November. https://www.pcisecuritystandards.org/pdfs/pr_111014_pts_v3-1.pdf

[5] Approved PIN Transaction Security Devices https://www.pcisecuritystandards.org/approved_companies_providers/approved_pin_transaction_security.p hp

[6] To help software vendors and others develop secure payment applications, the Council maintains the Payment Application Data Security Standard (PA-DSS). https://www.pcisecuritystandards.org/security_standards/documents.php?association=PA-DSS

[7] The PCI Security Standards Council offers robust and comprehensive standards and supporting materials to enhance payment card data security. These materials include a framework of specifications, tools, measurements and support resources to help organizations ensure the safe handling of cardholder information at every step. The keystone is the PCI Data Security Standard (PCI DSS), which provides an actionable framework for developing a robust payment card data security process -- including prevention, detection and appropriate reaction to security incidents. https://www.pcisecuritystandards.org/security_standards/documents.php?document=pci_dss_v2-0#pci_dss_v2-0

[8] List of Validated Payment Applications https://www.pcisecuritystandards.org/ approved_companies_providers/vpa_agreement.php

[9] PCI Security Standards Council. 2011. "PCI Security Standards Council Update on PA-DSS and Mobile Payment Acceptance Applications." Statement, June. https://www.pcisecuritystandards.org/documents/statement_110624_pcissc.pdf

[10] PCI Security Standards Council. 2011. "Which Applications are Eligible for PA-DSS Validation? A Guiding Checklist." Factsheet, June. https://www.pcisecuritystandards.org/documents/which_applications_eligible_for_pa-dss_validation.pdf

In: Mobile Financial Services　　　　　　ISBN: 978-1-62618-703-0
Editor: Silas Paulsen　　　　　　　　© 2013 Nova Science Publishers, Inc.

Chapter 8

TESTIMONY OF ED MCLAUGHLIN, CHIEF EMERGING PAYMENTS OFFICER, MASTERCARD WORLDWIDE. HEARING ON "THE FUTURE OF MONEY: HOW MOBILE PAYMENTS COULD CHANGE FINANCIAL SERVICES"*

Good morning, Chairman Capito, Ranking Member Maloney, and Members of the Subcommittee.

My name is Ed McLaughlin, and I am Chief Emerging Payments Officer at MasterCard Worldwide ("MasterCard") in Purchase, New York. It is my pleasure to appear before you today to discuss developments in mobile payments. The subject of this hearing is a fascinating one, and is on the cutting edge of what is driving change in the way consumers and businesses interact to complete transactions.

MasterCard is at the forefront of innovation in this space and a thought leader in mobile payments. We greatly appreciate the opportunity to be here today to share our perspective on how mobile payments are developing and benefitting consumers and businesses.

---

* This is an edited, reformatted and augmented version of the testimony given on March 22, 2012 before the House Committee on Finanical Services, Subcommittee on Financial Institutions and Consumer Credit.

MasterCard Is a Global Payments and Technology Company

MasterCard is a global payments and technology company that connects billions of consumers, thousands of financial institutions, and millions of merchants, governments and businesses worldwide, enabling them to use electronic forms of payment instead of cash and checks. MasterCard has been a leader in the transformation of mobile phones into secure mobile payment devices. We are pioneering the development of unique mobile information services to facilitate and promote financial inclusion and commerce, and we continue to be a champion of global mobile payment standards. MasterCard also operates the industry's only fully integrated global payment processing platform, which sets the standard for reliability, agility, flexibility, and security. Our platform and technology are fueling a global migration away from cash by enabling safer, less expensive, and more convenient ways for consumers to pay and for merchants to get paid. And, we are proud to be leading this migration by utilizing our assets and resources based right here in the U.S.

MasterCard's technology center, based in O'Fallon, Missouri, drives the software systems and operational network that enables us to seamlessly process billions of transactions representing trillions of dollars each year. Our electronic payment network has the capacity to handle more than 160 million transactions per hour with an average network response time of 130 milliseconds. This is more than twice as fast as our largest competitor. In 2011 alone, MasterCard processed 27.3 billion electronic payments totaling approximately $3.2 trillion, and nearly all of these transactions were processed in our U.S. facility. Through the efforts of MasterCard and other domestic companies, the U.S. is leading a new era of global commerce that will drive value to all participants, deliver greater personal financial empowerment, and offer additional possibilities for paying for goods and services and transferring money to the more than seven billion inhabitants of the globe.

It is an exciting time to be in the payments business, and at MasterCard we are working hard to drive innovations that deliver value to consumers, merchants, and our financial institution customers.

A WORLD DRIVEN BY DEVICES

Perhaps the best way to begin a conversation about what is going on in mobile payments is to acknowledge that there are transformations in consumer behaviors that are happening globally, and these transformations are driven in large part by near ubiquitous access to the Internet, social connectivity, and mobility. We have all seen this in our everyday life, and these trends in technology will continue to rapidly transform commerce. Given the popularity of the mobile phone (more than 4 billion subscribers worldwide), the personal nature of the device (most are carried at all times), and the capabilities of the device (data access, storage, and transfer), it is no wonder that mobile phones are rapidly becoming a popular channel for accessing financial services in-store and online. Mobile phones—and especially smart phones— are giving consumers who already use payment cards a better payment experience.

By some estimates there will be twice the number of connected devices as people globally by 2015. These devices are bringing changes to the way people interact and also to how they want to transact. For example, the acceptance of card-based payments through the use of a handheld device is opening up channels of transactions for entrepreneurs that were not possible a few years ago.

Regardless of the payment environment or device, we need to constantly focus on two goals—making paying for something as simple and compelling as possible for every participant in the payments chain while providing the highest levels of security to consumers, merchants, and our financial institution customers. Intelligent devices such as smart phones provide the opportunity to move both objectives in a positive direction simultaneously, and we invest heavily in technologies that make this duality possible.

As you might expect, smart phones are now providing a platform for the delivery of new applications that are transforming the in-store shopping experience. In a recent survey, over 50% of smart phone users have already used their phone to assist them in shopping in some way. In developed markets like the U.S., smart phones will soon represent over half of the mobile phones in the market. Smart phones provide consumers with the convenience of messaging, browsing, and applications that facilitate commerce. For merchants, smart phones provide a convenient channel to engage consumers at multiple levels, such as though an Internet store-front or a Facebook account, so that merchants can be available to consumers in all of the places where consumers want to find them.

Smart phones themselves are also becoming payment devices through the adoption of Near Field Communication, or NFC, technology. Indeed, major handset manufacturers, including Samsung, HTC, Nokia, and RIM are beginning to deliver NFC-enabled handsets to market, and by 2016 the majority of smart phones will support NFC. MasterCard's *PayPass* technology, which is discussed below, is central to the use of smart phones as payment devices.

Why are these new uses for mobile phones so important? Because they provide convenience and promote financial inclusion in a secure environment. Unlike the simple plastic card that has been around for decades, smart phones provide an intelligent device right in the consumer's hands that the consumer can use to interact with financial services providers and merchants in ways that were never before possible. For example, not only can smart phones provide faster and more convenient ways for consumers to pay, but they can also now enable consumers to access their account information before making a purchase to determine if the transaction is something the consumer can afford. This type of on-the-go budget tool will make more consumers comfortable using mainstream financial products. Smart phones also enable micro-entrepreneurs to accept payment card transactions, bringing more people into the payment system and empowering small businesses. For example, Square reported late last year that over 750,000 merchants are now using its smart phone technology to accept electronic payments. Companies like Intuit and iZettle also compete in this space for payment card acceptance.

FINANCIAL INCLUSION

When you look at the 85% of transactions that are still being funded through cash and check, emerging technologies such as smart phones provide an unprecedented opportunity to accelerate the transition to electronic payments and to enhance the lives of consumers, merchants, and communities around the world.

In this regard, we are particularly excited about the global movement towards mobile money. Mobile money creates a unique engine for financial inclusion. By enhancing the reach of our network and services to benefit consumers, we are now able to reach a large number of consumers who are outside the financial mainstream. For example, in markets in Latin America, Africa, and Asia, mobile network operators and financial institutions are increasingly providing access to financial services to the underserved through mobile devices, and MasterCard is working with our partners in these markets to use the assets of our network to help facilitate payments and replace cash. This is particularly so in those markets where the penetration of point of sale terminals that can read plastic cards may be very low.

One example of such collaboration can be seen in MasterCard's recent work with Airtel Africa and Standard Chartered Bank on the Airtel Card. The Airtel Card enables unbanked, underbanked and fully banked Airtel Money mobile wallet customers to conduct on-line shopping on any Internet site that accepts MasterCard in a secure and convenient way through use of single-use virtual debit cards. The Airtel Card received the award for Best Mobile Money Product or Solution at the 2011 GSMA Mobile Money Congress, where the judges commented that the Airtel Card "provides a developed-world service to the developing world with great use of existing and readily accessible technologies (such as MasterCard's network) to open up commerce and banking to the unbanked and underbanked."

We also believe that payment card solutions like prepaid cards coupled with mobile technology can unlock the global commerce grid to consumers who currently do not have access to financial services. The platforms we have created enable consumers without a traditional bank account to deposit money with a regulated entity or its agent to send money to family members in a distant town or to pay a bill across town, a feat that may have required consumers in the past to travel many miles or to take time off from work. In short, consumers now have new opportunities to access online commerce, transfer funds, pay bills and more. Continuing to invest in our networks will ensure that transactions such as these are made in record time and deliver the most efficient benefits to consumers and businesses alike.

MASTERCARD'S ROLE IN MOBILE PAYMENTS

As established commerce continues to migrate to new experiences, and newer markets such as digital media goods expand, we are moving not only to a world beyond cash, we are also starting to enable a world beyond plastic. This creates an incredible opportunity for MasterCard and others in the payments business to serve consumers with new experiences and to create value for merchants and other partners who deliver technology-based services to consumers, such as Google and Intel.

At MasterCard, we have invested substantial financial resources and human capital in developing the technology necessary for the mobile payments ecosystem. These efforts have focused on three areas. The first of these is what I will call a contactless-based system. MasterCard's *PayPass* "tap-and-go" product is at the forefront of this space. The second area of the mobile payments ecosystem we are seeing develop is based around SMS-based money management systems, which involve text messaging between mobile devices. MasterCard's MoneySend product is an example of this type of system. Third, as I have already mentioned, we are seeing exciting developments in mobile commerce-enabled systems with the rapid deployment of smart phones, including the innovative MasterCard *inControl* platform.

MasterCard *PayPass*. MasterCard's *PayPass* technology is a contactless payment method that enables consumers to pay with a payment product but without swiping a card. MasterCard has been building the *PayPass* infrastructure over the last decade, focusing on interoperability standards, acceptance locations, security and developing devices. *PayPass* is designed to displace cash for everyday purchases, and enhance credit, debit and prepaid payment products. A tiny microchip and radio antenna embedded in a *PayPass*-enabled card, key fob, device or phone transmit a customer's payment details wirelessly to a high-speed *PayPass* reader at checkout. The reader then verifies the transaction with the customer's bank through the MasterCard network and indicates approval almost instantly.

Encryption technology and MasterCard's Zero Liability protection on a *PayPass*-enabled credit, debit or prepaid MasterCard card make using *PayPass* at checkout as safe as swiping. *PayPass* also has built-in safeguards to help prevent unwanted purchases—it never leaves a customer's hands at checkout, it must be very close to the card reader for it to work, and it only bills the customer once, even if it is tapped twice. As we continue to develop the *PayPass* program, MasterCard is committed to expanding merchant acceptance in key categories, developing contactless payments for transit, working to expand functionality to mobile phones and other options, expanding beyond low-value payment channels, and increasing marketplace awareness and education. By linking a mobile phone to MasterCard *PayPass*, we bring a new level of convenience to consumers by enabling them to tap and go at any of our contactless- enabled merchants around the globe with the reliability and protections of all MasterCard transactions.

Mobile MoneySend. MoneySend is MasterCard's fully-integrated, on-demand person-to- person mobile payment platform for financial institutions that issue MasterCard products in the United States. Mobile MoneySend is a breakthrough payment platform that provides a better way for consumers to send and receive funds via SMS-text, mobile browser, mobile applet or an

Internet PC. Once consumers are registered for MoneySend with their bank, the consumers have the flexibility of directly, easily and securely transferring funds to and from one another through their mobile phone, eliminating the need to write or cash checks, visit ATMs, or wire money domestically.

Senders initiate transfers to any domestic mobile phone number via SMS message, mobile web browser or a downloadable MoneySend application. Upon initiation of the transfer, the sender approves the request by entering the MoneySend mobile PIN which only the accountholder knows. The recipient receives a text message confirmation of the transfer (for pre-registered users) or that the transfer is pending (for yet to be registered users). The funds can then be accessed by the recipient through an account designated during the registration process. These funds are then available for access through the mobile phone. If the consumer has a MasterCard card associated with the account, the funds can also be accessed at traditional points of interaction, including ATMs, over-the-counter at a bank branch, or at the point-of-sale.

MasterCard *inControl*. MasterCard *inControl* is an innovative platform that offers an array of advanced authorization, transaction routing and alert controls to satisfy consumer demand for increased security and budgeting capability. With *inControl*, spending limits and controls can be set on payment accounts to enable account owners to determine exactly where, when and how their cards are used. Coupled with these controls, real-time email or text alerts can be sent to account owners to provide transparency into the spending activity occurring on the account. For consumers, *inControl* provides a new level of financial control and awareness that is unmatched in today's market. Cardholders create personalized spending profiles for themselves and their family members by setting up spending limits according to budget goals and account security concerns. Cardholders can also choose to receive real-time alerts on specific transactions as well as when spending is nearing a budgeted amount. Because of our substantial investment in innovations like *inControl*, consumers can harness their mobile phones in ways that enables them to manage their finances more efficiently and spend with greater confidence.

PROTECTING CONSUMERS AND DELIVERING VALUE

As I mentioned at the outset, we are driven to make payments simple for all participants in the payments value chain, while providing the highest levels of security. This is why we apply MasterCard's Zero Liability protections to new payment technologies, including mobile phone-based payments. The

MasterCard Zero Liability policy offers MasterCard cardholders peace of mind, as in most instances they are not liable in the event of the unauthorized use of a MasterCard-branded product.

Another way we deliver value to participants in the MasterCard network is to ensure that transactions are processed seamlessly and to take steps to combat payment card fraud before it occurs. These are top priorities for MasterCard. We have consistently maintained availability of our global processing systems more than 99.9% of the time. We are able to do this because our network provides multiple levels of back-up protection and related continuity procedures. Moreover, our network features multiple layers of protection against hacking or other cybersecurity attacks, which we supplement with mitigation efforts to strengthen our protection against such threats, both in terms of operability of the network and protection of the information transmitted through the network.

As data is increasingly stored in electronic formats, preventing fraud is more important than ever. Recognizing the importance to cardholders, financial institutions, and merchants of the security of payment card information, and the consumer and other harms that flow from the fraudulent and unauthorized use of such information, MasterCard helped lead the industry in developing the Payment Card Industry Data Security Standard ("PCI DSS"). The PCI DSS is managed by an open governance body, the PCI Security Standards Council, of which all the major payment card brands are members.

The PCI DSS includes requirements for security management, policies, procedures, network architecture, software design and other critical protective measures. The PCI DSS is intended to help organizations proactively protect payment card account data. We operate several compliance programs in connection with the PCI DSS and otherwise to help ensure that the integrity of our payment system is maintained by our customers and their agents. Key compliance programs include merchant audits (for high fraud, excessive chargebacks and processing of illegal transactions) and security compliance (including our MasterCard Site Data Protection Service®, which assists customers and merchants in protecting commercial sites from hacker intrusions and subsequent account data compromises) by requiring proper adherence to the PCI DSS. Our customers are also required to report instances of fraud to us in a timely manner so we can monitor trends and initiate action where appropriate. MasterCard continues to work with the PCI Security Standards Council as it develops standards to protect payment card account data in an increasingly mobile world.

In furtherance of our efforts to attack fraud and ensure the integrity of payment transactions on our network, we have recently announced a program to transition MasterCard- branded payment products in the U.S. to the EMV standard. The EMV standard is a global standard for credit and debit payment cards based on chip technology, the objective of which is to ensure interoperability and acceptance of payment cards on a worldwide basis. The adoption of EMV-compliant payment products in the U.S. will help provide additional layers of protection for consumers at the point of interaction, enabling dynamic authentication across all channels and devices—card, smart phone or otherwise.

CONCLUSION

MasterCard is extremely proud of the role we play in advancing commerce through new technologies. The rise of the mobile phone, and other smart handheld wireless devices, is transforming the way we conduct our everyday lives, and holds significant promise for delivering new value to consumers and businesses in the delivery of financial services. As I said at the outset, it is an exciting time to be in the payments business.

I appreciate the opportunity to appear before you today and I will be glad to answer any questions you may have.

In: Mobile Financial Services
Editor: Silas Paulsen
ISBN: 978-1-62618-703-0
© 2013 Nova Science Publishers, Inc.

Chapter 9

TESTIMONY OF RANDY VANDERHOOF, EXECUTIVE DIRECTOR, SMART CARD ALLIANCE. HEARING ON "THE FUTURE OF MONEY: HOW MOBILE PAYMENTS COULD CHANGE FINANCIAL SERVICES"*

Chairwoman Capito and Members of the Subcommittee:

On behalf of the Smart Card Alliance and its members, I thank you for the opportunity to testify today. The Smart Card Alliance is a non-profit organization that provides education and a collaborative, open forum among leaders in various industries including mobile payments. The Alliance represents many major stakeholders in the mobile payments ecosystem including payment brands, card issuers, mobile operators, merchants, and technology providers.

We applaud the Subcommittee's leadership and foresight in examining important issues essential to making mobile payments safe, flexible and resilient with the appropriate legal, regulatory and security frameworks.

The number of American wireless subscriber connections now exceeds the population of the United States and its territories according to industry sources. The total population is 315.5 million inhabitants, while the number of wireless subscriber connections is 327.6 million. Of these, 96 million, almost

---

* This is an edited, reformatted and augmented version of the testimony given on March 22, 2012 before the House Committee on Finnical Services, Subcommittee on Financial Institutions and Consumer Credit.

one out of three, are smartphones and wireless-enabled PDAs that are capable of accessing the Internet and doing much of what people do on their PCs.[1]

Over the course of the last ten years, the mobile phone has become the thing people don't leave home without. So it's not surprising that everyone— especially consumers— want to use it for payment and mobile commerce too. Industry forecasts suggest m- commerce is expected to grow 73% in 2012 to $11.6 billion.[2]

The 2011 report published by the Federal Reserve Banks of Boston and Atlanta through their Retail Payments Risk Forum points out correctly that there are many ways mobile devices can be used to facilitate the payment process.[3] I am going to focus my remarks on just one area that is getting a lot of attention, which is the use of a payment application-enabled mobile phone with a mobile virtual wallet inside that can be used to pay at a physical merchant location as a substitute for a credit or debit card.

This hearing was convened to examine issues essential to making mobile payments safe and to ensure appropriate legislative oversight is in place.

The good news is that for the type of mobile payments that I am talking about, which is using your mobile phone like a payment card, there is a clear mobile technology path forward that achieves these goals because this form of mobile payment is built on already established legal, regulatory and security frameworks in both the payment and wireless telecom industries. In the industry, this mobile technology is referred to as NFC mobile contactless payment. NFC, or Near Field Communication, is a form of short range wireless communications inside a phone.

NFC is a new technology that leverages many layers of existing smart card technology in payment cards (EMV and contactless cards) and wireless mobile devices (SIM cards) and that, together with the existing payment and wireless network infrastructure, enable secure mobile payment at physical merchant locations equipped with NFC-compatible POS terminals.

The NFC mobile contactless payment approach has two advantages very important to this Subcommittee. First, underpinning the legal and regulatory framework is the simple fact that while NFC mobile payments use a phone instead of a card, the payment account remains a credit or debit card account and, as such, is already well-protected for consumers and industry stakeholders by existing laws and regulations. Second, the security and reliability of this approach are grounded in global standards, established certification processes and industry best practices that are the culmination of nearly 20 years of work in applying smart card technology to protect payment accounts and mobile phone subscribers.

I would like to stress that the major stakeholders and technology providers in the financial and mobile industries have been collaborating for years across multiple global standards organizations to add NFC mobile contactless payments to their existing payment and wireless infrastructures. These include:

- NFC Forum, a global standards organization whose members include the leading global payment brands and wireless technology providers
- EMVCo and GlobalPlatform, the former managing the global payments standards for the use of smart card chips in bank cards and now also in phones; and the latter setting standards that facilitate secure and interoperable applications using smart card chip technology in cards and phones, with members including the leading global payment brands and payment technology providers
- The GSM Association (GSMA), consisting of 800 mobile operators and related companies and devoted to supporting and standardizing wireless mobile telephone systems worldwide
- ETSI, the telecommunications standards organization

These organizations have developed the standards for NFC, which are supported by the mobile industry and endorsed by the payments industry, who then applied their own standards, best practices, certification procedures and compliance testing to ensure secure and interoperable NFC mobile contactless payments. The resulting NFC mobile payments ecosystem is safe, flexible and resilient.

The fact that leading payment brands are involved will not only ensure security, it will create trust by consumers and accelerate rapid adoption. According to a recent independent branding study, the brands most trusted by consumers for protecting mobile payments are Visa, MasterCard and American Express.[4]

I'd like to go a little deeper into what NFC is, how it fits into the payments and telecom ecosystems, and why it is secure. NFC technology is implemented in a chipset embedded in mobile phones that enables consumers to transact at a physical point of sale. The technology leverages added security features in the mobile phone and includes something called a "secure element,"[5] a smart chip protecting the sensitive payment data stored inside the phone as well as managing the execution of the payment transaction by the consumer. In addition, new and existing safeguards in the wireless and payment networks are used with mobile payment devices to add many layers of protection for consumer account information and transactions. For example, access to the payment application can be password protected and a lost or stolen phone can be turned off instantly with one call to the mobile operator who services that customer.

The Smart Card Alliance has created an educational white paper, "Security of Proximity Mobile Payments," that discusses this subject in detail.[6]

An NFC-enabled phone is provisioned with a version of a payment application (e.g., American Express ExpressPay, Discover Zip, MasterCard PayPass, Visa payWave) and personalized with a payment account (i.e., credit , debit or prepaid) issued by the consumer's financial institution.

To pay, the consumer simply holds or taps the phone close to the merchant's reader. The consumer's account information is sent to the contactless POS reader via radio frequency. The payment and settlement processes are the same processes used when a consumer pays with a traditional contactless or magnetic stripe credit or debit card.

Market development involving many of America's largest and most trusted companies is well underway. One example using the NFC mobile contactless payment technology standards we are discussing here is Isis. This mobile carrier joint venture includes AT&T, Verizon Wireless, and T-Mobile and will work with American Express, Discover, MasterCard, and Visa for its NFC rollouts.

Another example is Google Wallet. Google has already launched its NFC mobile contactless payments offering to consumers, partnering in its initial launch with MasterCard, Citi, First Data, and Sprint. More than two dozen large retailers, including Macy's and American Eagle Outfitters have enabled their stores to accept Google Wallet.

Mobile payments are likely to grow quickly, aided by the rapid rate at which consumers replace their mobile phones with newer technology. Industry watcher Juniper Research predicts NFC payments will hit $74 billion by 2015.[7] Sales of NFC handsets in 2012 will reach nearly 80 million units, an increase of 129% from 2011, according to IMS Research.[8]

In summary "the future of money," as this hearing is entitled, is being positively impacted by mobile technology. The changes in financial services that you have rightfully called attention to with this hearing are being well-managed and securely protected by the technology and the collective knowledge and resources of the financial and mobile industries.

NFC, the core technology behind mobile contactless payments, was chosen by the mobile carriers and financial industry as the delivery mechanism due to its security and ease of use. The consumer payments applications have been jointly developed on the mobile side by the four largest mobile network brands and on the payments side by the four payments brands, which, according to consumers who were surveyed, were the most trusted for mobile payments in the United States. The path forward has been paved by years of experience.

NFC payment embedded in mobile phones won't be the only form of mobile payment, but this way forward is based on known elements and backed by the mobile operators and payment brands. There are new mobile technologies being tested other than NFC that are promising, yet unproven.

NFC offers many benefits to consumers, both to make payments more convenient and to support new, innovative capabilities that deliver value to both consumers and merchants. Confidence in the underlying infrastructure and credibility of the industry offerings are critical to consumer adoption. Consumers will benefit from a mobile payments infrastructure that is based on a proven set of standards and architectures, has a strong focus on security, and uses the existing payments infrastructure for transactions.

Mobile phones offer a powerful computing platform for innovation and represent a fertile landscape for new ways for consumers to transact with retailers, financial institutions, application stores and each other. Mobile payments innovation is going to continue to evolve and as more people upgrade to smartphones and learn about all of the new services they hold in the palm of their hand. An added benefit of the migration to NFC will be the fact that mobile devices will generally become more secure, because the security technology needed for payment can be used safely for other applications as well.

CONCLUSION

To sum up, NFC contactless mobile payments as planned by the financial services and wireless industries are basically credit and debit accounts that fit within the legal, regulatory and security frameworks that are serving the public interest today.

The Smart Card Alliance would like to thank the Subcommittee once again for holding this important and forward-looking hearing. Government and industry must maintain an open dialog about legal, regulatory and security frameworks and we greatly appreciate the opportunity to present information that assists in developing options for making mobile payments a reality; in addressing the challenges and opportunities of using mobile payment systems to exchange value; and in setting the legal, regulatory and security frameworks necessary to implement a safe, flexible and resilient mobile financial product.

We have provided appendices at the end of this written statement to further assist you in examining the mobile landscape as it stands today.

APPENDIX A. NFC MOBILE CONTACTLESS PAYMENT

NFC Basics

NFC stands for Near Field Communication and is a standards-based wireless communication technology that allows data to be exchanged between devices that are a few centimeters apart. The technology can be used for a wide variety of mobile applications, including:

- Making payments with a wave or a touch of a device anywhere contactless point-of-sale readers have been deployed
- Reading information and picking up special offers, coupons, and discounts from posters or billboards on which an RF tag has been embedded (for example, in smart posters and billboards)
- Securely storing tickets for transportation, parking access, or events and enabling fast transactions at the point of entry/exit
- Securely storing information that allows secure building access

An NFC-enabled device[9] can operate in different modes to implement a wide variety mobile applications, including mobile contactless payment.

NFC Mobile Contactless Payment

Contactless payment -- payment with the use of contactless debt and credit cards – has been a growing market over the past several years. American Express, Discover, MasterCard and Visa branded cards are being issued that contain smart chips that enable contactless payment. The contactless merchant point-of-sale infrastructure that is now in place to support credit and debit payment can also accept NFC mobile contactless payments, providing a head-start for broad acceptance and use.

With NFC, contactless payment capabilities are in the mobile phone, allowing secure storage and use of payment accounts with the mobile phone.

To support mobile contactless payments, the NFC-enabled phone has a smart chip (called the "secure element") which is loaded with a version of a payment application (e.g., American Express ExpressPay, Discover Zip, MasterCard PayPass, Visa payWave) and personalized with a payment account (i.e., credit, debit or prepaid) issued by the consumer's financial institution.

The phone can then use NFC technology to communicate with a merchant's contactless payment-capable POS system. To pay, the consumer simply holds or taps the phone close to the merchant's reader. The consumer's account information is sent to the contactless POS reader via radio frequency. The payment and settlement processes are the same processes used when a consumer pays with a traditional contactless or magnetic stripe credit or debit card.

Currently many NFC mobile payment pilots and initiatives are happening worldwide involving many of the world's largest companies. Most notably in the U.S., Google Wallet is currently available to owners of the Nexus S 4G on Sprint Mobile, and Isis, the joint venture among AT&T Mobility, Verizon Wireless, and T-Mobile USA, has signed up American Express, Discover, MasterCard, and Visa for NFC mobile payments.

The figure below illustrates the security mechanisms that protect the processes used in NFC mobile contactless payments; these mechanisms are described below.

Delivering Financial Data Securely

The issuer transmits payment, personalization, and life cycle management information to a Trusted Service Manager (TSM) using standard Internet technologies, such as secure sockets layer (SSL) or virtual private networks (VPNs).

GlobalPlatform's secure channel protocol provides for transmission of sensitive account data between the TSM and the secure element in the mobile device and for storage of the information in the phone's secure element. Account data is further kept secure by encryption provided by the mobile network operator (MNO).

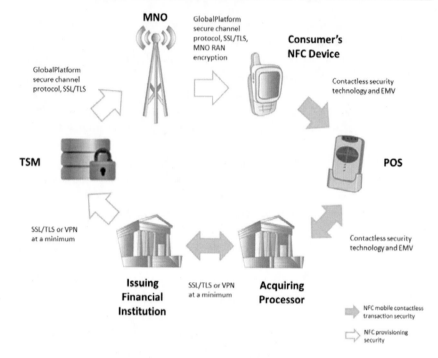

Figure 1. NFC Mobile Contactless Payments Security Mechanisms.

Protecting Stored Payment Application and Account Information

Within the mobile phone, both the payment application and consumer account information must be protected, and different NFC applications must be able to work securely and independently of each other. Security approaches used include:

- Storing the payment application and data in the secure element.
- Using smart card technology that is inherent in the secure element to authenticate all communications with applications and to provide built-in tamper resistance.
- Providing a mobile wallet for accessing the payment account information in the secure element during a transaction, with an optional personal identification number (PIN) authorizing access to the wallet.

Protecting the Payment Transaction

When the consumer uses the NFC device for payment, the transaction is protected using the same security mechanisms in place for contactless credit and debit cards. Payments are processed over the current financial networks and use the payments industry security infrastructure. Security approaches used include:

- Leveraging existing issuer host system payment transaction authorization technology and account management processes.
- Protecting the transaction using the dynamic cryptogram authentication technology that is already in place for contactless credit and debit cards.
- Leveraging EMV contactless card transaction authentication security technology.

NFC and EMV

The global payments industry is migrating to the next generation payments infrastructure based on smart chip technology and the EMV specifications[10]. EMV is an open-standard set of specifications for payments and acceptance devices using smart chip technology. The EMV specifications were developed to address issues with fraud in the magnetic stripe infrastructure and to define a set of requirements to ensure interoperability between smart chip-based payment cards and terminals.

The U.S. is now starting its migration to EMV, with recent announcements by Discover, MasterCard and Visa detailing their roadmaps for issuers, acquirers/processors and merchants. The payment brands' roadmaps were developed to accelerate adoption of both EMV and mobile contactless payments.

For NFC mobile contactless payments, the mobile phone's secure element will be provisioned with the payment brands' EMV application and work with the same EMV contactless point-of-sale readers being put in place globally.

NFC mobile contactless payment transactions between a mobile phone and a POS terminal use the same communications protocol currently used by EMV and U.S. contactless credit and debit cards. This means that consumers can use their NFC- enabled mobile phones for payment at the existing installed base of contactless credit and debit terminals that are based on the EMV standard.

NFC Mobile Contactless Payments: Looking Forward

Globally, the mobile telecommunications industry and the financial payments industry have shown significant commitment to the deployment of NFC mobile contactless payments – not only fielding numerous trials and pilots but also collaborating on the development of the standards, architectures, best practices and security approaches for NFC mobile contactless payments to ensure a secure, interoperable mobile payments infrastructure.[11] This broad industry commitment and collaboration make NFC mobile contactless payments unique among the different mobile payments approaches.

NFC offers many benefits to consumers, both to make payments more convenient and to support new, innovative capabilities that deliver value to both the consumer and to merchants. Confidence in the underlying infrastructure and credibility of the industry offerings are critical to consumer adoption. Consumers will benefit from a mobile payments infrastructure that is based on a proven set of standards and architectures, has a strong focus on security, and uses the existing payments infrastructure for transactions.

References and Resources

- EMV Frequently Asked Questions - http://www.smartcardalliance.org/pages/publications-emv-faq
- EMV Resources - http://www.smartcardalliance.org/pages/smart-cards-applications-emv
- Google Wallet – http://www.google.com/wallet/
- Isis – http://www.paywithisis.com/
- "MasterCard Introduces U.S. Roadmap to Enable Next Generation of Electronic Payments," January 30, 2012, http://www.smartcardalliance.org/articles/2012/01/31/mastercard-introduces-u-s-roadmap-to-enable-next-generation-of-electronic-payments-january-30-2012-framework- to-deliver-enhanced-consumer-experience-in-store-online-at-the-atm-and-with-mobile- phones

- "The Mobile Payments and NFC Landscape: A U.S. Perspective," Smart Card Alliance white paper, September 2011, http://www. smartcardalliance.org/resources/pdf/Mobile_Payments_White_Paper_ 091611.pdf
- NFC Forum – http://www.nfc-forum.org
- NFC Trial and Pilots, NFC World, http://www.nfcworld.com/list-of-nfc-trials-pilots-tests- and-commercial-services-around-the-world/
- "Security of Proximity Mobile Payments, Smart Card Alliance white paper," May 2009, http://www.smartcardalliance.org/resources/pdf/ Security_of_Proximity_Mobile_Payment s.pdf
- NFC Frequently Asked Questions - http://www.smartcardalliance.org/ pages/publications- nfc-frequently-asked-questionsNFC Resources - http://www.smartcardalliance.org/pages/smart-cards-applications-nfc
- Smart Card Alliance – http://www.smartcardalliance.org
- "Visa Announces Plans to Accelerate Chip Migration and Adoption of Mobile Payments," August 9, 2011 -- http://www. smartcardalliance. org/articles/2011/08/09/visa-announces-plans-to-accelerate-chip-migration-and-adoption-of-mobile-payments

APPENDIX B. GLOSSARY

Chip

An electronic component that performs logic, processing, and/or memory functions.

Contactless Payments

Payment transactions that require no physical contact between the consumer's payment device and the physical POS terminal. The consumer holds the contactless card or other device less than 2-4 inches from the merchant POS terminal, and the payment account information is communicated wirelessly via radio frequency (RF).

CTIA

International industry association representing the wireless communications industry.

ECMA International

Industry association founded in 1961 and dedicated to the standardization of information and communication technology and consumer electronics. ECMA is active in defining standards for Near Field Communication.

EMV

Europay MasterCard Visa. Specifications developed by Europay, MasterCard and Visa that define a set of requirements to ensure interoperability between payment chip cards and terminals.

EMVCo

The organization formed in February 1999 by Europay International, MasterCard International, and Visa International to manage, maintain, and enhance the EMV Integrated Circuit Card Specifications for Payment Systems. EMVCo is currently owned by American Express, JCB, MasterCard Worldwide, and Visa, Inc.

ETSI

European Telecommunications Standards Institute. Organization that produces globally- applicable standards for information and communications technologies, including fixed, mobile, radio, converged, broadcast and Internet technologies.

Global Platform

An international, non-profit association, with the mission to establish, maintain and drive adoption of standards to enable an open and interoperable infrastructure for smart cards, devices and systems that simplifies and accelerates development, deployment and management of applications across industries.

GSMA

Industry association that represents the interests of mobile operators worldwide and includes a broad set of companies in the broader mobile ecosystem.

IC

Integrated circuit.

Issuer

The bank that provides a credit card to a cardholder.

IEC

International Electrotechnical Commission. A standards organization for electrical, electronic and related technologies.

ISO

International Organization for Standardization. A non-governmental organization that is a network of national standards institutes of 163 countries, with a central secretariat that coordinates the system.

Mobile Contactless Payments

A payment to a physical merchant that is initiated from an NFC-enabled mobile phone held in close proximity (within a few centimeters) of the merchant's POS equipment.

Mobile Network Operator (MNO)

The mobile telecommunications company that has the relationship and mobile phone account with the end user.

Mobile Proximity Payments

Mobile payment transaction in which a consumer uses a phone to pay for goods or services at a physical POS.

Mobile Remote Payments

Mobile payment transactions in which consumers use a smartphone or mobile phone to make purchases without interacting with a physical POS.

Mobile Wallet

A software application that is loaded onto a mobile phone to manage payments made from the mobile phone. A mobile wallet application can also hold and control a number of other applications (for example, payment and loyalty), much as a physical wallet holds a collection of physical cards.

Near Field Communication (NFC)

A standards-based wireless communication technology that allows data to be exchanged between devices that are a few centimeters apart. NFC-enabled mobile phones incorporate a smart chip (called a *secure element*) that allows the phone to store the payment application and consumer account information securely and use the information as a virtual payment card. NFC payment transactions between a mobile phone and a POS terminal use the standard ISO/IEC 14443 communication protocol currently used by EMV and U.S. contactless credit and debit cards.

NFC Forum

Industry association that was formed to advance the use of Near Field Communication technology by developing specifications, ensuring interoperability among devices and services, and educating the market about NFC technology.

OTA (Over-the-Air)

The possibility to send data to and receive data from a mobile device in a distributed environment. In GSM networks, OTA can use a data connection or SMS.

Personalization

The process of incorporating the unique personal data for a user into a generic device or card.

PIN (Personal Identification Number)

The numeric code associated with a payment account or card that adds a second factor of authentication to the identity verification process.

POS (Point-of-Sale)

The merchant's physical location where the payment transaction takes place. This term is also used to describe the equipment used by the merchant to complete the payment transaction.

Reader

Any device that transmits data or assists in data transmission between a card, token, or other device and a host computer or database.

Smart Card

A device that includes an embedded secure integrated circuit that can be either a secure microcontroller or equivalent intelligence with internal memory or a secure memory chip alone. The card connects to a reader with direct physical contact or with a remote contactless radio frequency interface. With an embedded microcontroller, smart cards have the unique ability to securely store large amounts of data, carry out their own on-card functions (e.g., encryption and mutual authentication), and interact intelligently with a smart card reader. Smart card technology conforms to international standards (ISO/IEC 7816 and ISO/IEC 14443) and is available in a variety of form factors, including plastic cards, subscriber identification modules (SIMs) used in GSM mobile phones, and USB-based tokens.

Smart Chip

The secure integrated circuit that is used in smart cards and other form factors. Smart chips are embedded in plastic cards, subscriber identification modules (SIMs) and secure elements used in mobile phones, and USB-based tokens.

Secure Element (SE)

The component in a mobile phone that provides security and confidentiality. A secure element can reside on the SIM, in a dedicated chip on a phone's motherboard (embedded secure element), or as an external accessory. The secure element is a smart card chip that contains a dedicated microprocessor with an operating system, memory, an application environment, and security protocols. It is used to store and execute sensitive applications on a mobile device.

Trusted Service Manager (TSM)

A neutral third party who provides a single integration point with mobile operators for financial institutions, and retailers who want to provide a payment, ticketing, loyalty or other NFC application to their customers with NFC-enabled phones.

End Notes

[1] CTIA - The Wireless Association, "CTIA-The Wireless Association Semi-Annual Survey Reveals Historical Wireless Trend," October 11, 2011 (http://www.ctia.org/media/press/body.cfm/prid/2133)

[2] eMarketer, "Smartphones Turn Millions More Americans into Mobile Shoppers," January 6, 2012 (http://www.emarketer.com/Article.aspx?R=1008769)

[3] "Mobile Payments in the United States: Mapping Out the Road Ahead," Darin Contini and Marianne Crowe, Federal Reserve Bank of Boston, Cynthia Merritt and Richard Oliver, Federal Reserve Bank of Atlanta, and Steve Mott, BetterBuyDesign, March 25, 2011

[4] Kunur Patel, "Survey: Consumers Don't Trust Google or Apple With Mobile Payments," AdAge, August 9, 2011 (http://adage.com/article/digital/consumers-trust-google-apple-mobile-payments/229163/)

[5] The component in a mobile phone that provides security and confidentiality. A secure element can reside on the SIM, in a dedicated chip on a phone's motherboard (embedded secure element), or as an external accessory. The secure element is a smart card chip that contains a dedicated microprocessor with an operating system, memory, an application environment, and security protocols. It is used to store and execute sensitive applications on a mobile device. Source: Smart Card Alliance, "Security of Proximity Mobile Payments," May 2009

[6] Smart Card Alliance, "Security of Proximity Mobile Payments," May 2009 (http://www.smartcardalliance.org/pages/publications-security-of-proximity-mobile-payments)

[7] Juniper Research, "Mobile Commerce Market Set to Accelerate with NFC Facilitating $74bn Transactions by 2015," March 8, 2012 (http://juniperresearch.com/viewpressrelease.php?pr=291)

[8] IMS Research, "35 Million Handsets in 2011 Marks Breakthrough Year for Mobile Near-Field Communications," December 14, 2011 (http://imsresearch.com/press-release/35_Million_Handsets_in_2011_Marks_Breakthrough_Year_for_Mobile_NearField_Communicatio ns)

[9] NFC-enabled devices are governed by standards in ISO/IEC (ISO/IEC 18092), ETSI (ETSI TS 102 10 V1.1.1 (2003-03)) and ECMA International (ECMA-340), and by specifications published by the NFC Forum.

[10] EMV stands for Europay MasterCard Visa, the three organizations who developed the initial specifications. The EMV specifications are now managed, maintained and enhanced by EMVCo.

[11] Organizations involved in the development of standards and best practices include: GSMA, ETSI, NFC Forum, Smart Card Alliance, Mobey Forum, GlobalPlatform, EMVCo.

In: Mobile Financial Services ISBN: 978-1-62618-703-0
Editor: Silas Paulsen © 2013 Nova Science Publishers, Inc.

Chapter 10

TESTIMONY OF SUZANNE MARTINDALE, STAFF ATTORNEY, CONSUMERS UNION. HEARING ON "THE FUTURE OF MONEY: HOW MOBILE PAYMENTS COULD CHANGE FINANCIAL SERVICES"*

Chairman Capito, Ranking Member Maloney and Members of the Committee, thank you for the opportunity to testify about mobile payments on behalf of Consumers Union, the advocacy and policy arm of *Consumer Reports®*.

"Mobile payments" allow consumers to buy products or transfer money with a mobile device. The market includes a range of different technologies, and many ways to fund transactions. The U.S. mobile payments market is still developing, and it remains unclear which trends will prevail. It is too soon to know which consumers will benefit most from the industry's growth – or, inversely, be most vulnerable to risk. However, policymakers can make a few simple fixes to ensure that mobile payments are safe.

The mobile payments market is, in a word, complex. There are multiple ways to initiate payments. Some services involve sending a text message, or using an application downloaded to the device. Others employ a chip embedded in the hardware, which the consumer waves at a contactless reader.

---

* This is an edited, reformatted and augmented version of the testimony given on March 22, 2012 before the House Committee on Finanical Services, Subcommittee on Financial Institutions and Consumer Credit.

Furthermore, multiple parties are involved in completing a transaction. Consumers, merchants, third-party processors, wireless carriers and financial institutions all play a role in the ecosystem. With so many players involved, the risk of confusion increases should something go wrong. Who is responsible for fixing a problem? If the different parties all point fingers at each other, the consumer may be out of luck.

Despite these challenges, mobile payments in the U.S. are projected to gross $214 billion by 2015,[1] in part due to their potential to provide speed and convenience for consumers and merchants.[2] Some merchants are also interested in the technology because mobile payment service providers may charge lower processing fees than traditional credit and debit card networks at the point of sale.[3]

Mobile payment technologies also have the potential to serve new audiences. They may appeal to young, tech-savvy consumers, as well as consumers who go outside the traditional banking system for financial services. For "unbanked" or "underbanked" consumers, mobile payments may provide increased access to financial services.[4] Low-income households and households of color in particular are more likely to be unbanked or underbanked.[5] Meanwhile, according to a recent Pew study, cell phone adoption is higher among households of color, as is smartphone adoption.[6] This presents an opportunity for mobile payment technologies to penetrate these markets. However, these same markets may be vulnerable to risk without adequate safeguards.

Internationally, mobile payments have garnered attention for helping consumers in developing countries gain access to financial services. An estimated 5 billion consumers worldwide have mobile phones, while only 1.5 billion have access to financial services.[7] In Kenya, where more consumers have cell phones than have bank accounts, Safaricom's popular M-PESA service enables consumers to manage transactions entirely through their mobile phones.[8] M-PESA customers can deposit or withdraw cash and send money through a network of agents and ATM machines, and can buy goods and services with their mobile phones – all without a bank account.[9]

However, U.S. consumers have been slow to adopt mobile payments, for several reasons. Some mobile payment systems remain limited in scope and availability. For example, the new Google Wallet uses an NFC (or near field communication) chip embedded in the mobile device, which the consumer waves at a contactless reader to make a payment. However, Google Wallet is only available to Sprint customers with a Nexus S smartphone.[10] Another mobile payments system, Bling Nation, uses a sticker with an embedded chip that the consumer affixes to the device and waves at a reader. However, Bling Nation is still available only through pilot programs in Palo Alto, Chicago and Austin.[11]

Furthermore, market research indicates that consumers have concerns about security of their financial information. In a survey released last week, the Federal Reserve found that over 40% of consumers cited security concerns as a reason for not using mobile payments.[12]

Finally, not all ways to pay with a mobile device are created equal when it comes to consumer protections. Although consumers may not be aware of it, U.S. payments law is fragmented. The level of protections against unauthorized transactions and errors varies depending on whether a consumer links payment to a credit card, debit card or bank account, prepaid card, prepaid phone deposit, or phone bill.[13] Traditional credit and debit cards have mandatory protections under existing law; however, prepaid cards do not.[14] Mobile payments linked to a prepaid phone deposit or phone bill are especially problematic, because they do not fit neatly into existing legal categories.[15] Wireless carriers may provide voluntary protections, but they are typically not disclosed in customer contracts.[16]

The different ways to pay by mobile device, and the varying consumer protections that apply to each, create the potential for confusion when a consumer is faced with a transaction gone wrong. Consumers need to know where to complain and how to get their money back in case of errors or unauthorized use. Consumers cannot afford to lose precious funds due to inadequate protections. For low- and moderate- income consumers, this loss could be especially acute.

Until U.S. payments law is updated to provide clear, guaranteed protections for all payment methods, consumers may be at risk when using mobile payments technology. Nonetheless, a few simple fixes could close gaps in protections and provide clarity to the industry. The Consumer Financial Protection Bureau (CFPB) is in a unique position to address mobile payments, because it has jurisdiction over payment service providers[17] and can clarify regulations implementing federal consumer financial laws.[18] Congress and other federal agencies also have an important role to play in establishing sensible rules of the road that protect consumers and foster innovation. Further dialogue between industry, regulators and consumers is the first step toward shaping a safe and thriving mobile payments market.

Thank you again for the opportunity to testify. I am happy to answer any of your questions.

End Notes

[1] Andrew Johnson, *In Mobile Payments, Lack of Interoperability Threatens Adoption*, AM. BANKER, Dec. 9, 2010, *available at* http://www.americanbanker.com/issues/175_235/lack-of-interoperability-1029690-1.html.

[2] *See, e.g.*, Kate Fitzgerald, Starbucks National Push for Mobile Payments, AM. BANKER, Dec. 6, 2010, *available at* http://www.americanbanker.com/issues/175_232/starbucks-mobile-payments-1029437-1.html. Starbucks' President of U.S. Operations, told *The American Banker* that using mobile payments technology at point of sale was part of their effort to move customers through checkout more quickly. *Id.*

[3] For example, Bling, a mobile payments service that uses contactless readers at the point of sale, charges a 1.5% transaction fee, about half the amount of the usual credit card fee on the merchant. Jefferson Graham, *Customers Pay By Smartphones, Not Credit Cards*, USA TODAY, Dec. 1, 2010, *available at* http://www.usatoday.com/tech/news/2010-12-01-mobilepayments01_ST_N.htm.

[4] The Federal Deposit Insurance Corporation (FDIC) reported in December 2009 that 25.6% of U.S. households, about 30 million, rely on non-banks for some or all of their financial services needs. FED. DEPOSIT INS. CORP., FDIC NATIONAL SURVEY OF UNBANKED AND UNDERBANKED HOUSEHOLDS 11 (2009), *available at* http://www.fdic.gov/householdsurvey/Full_Report.pdf.

[5] *Id.* at 10-11.

[6] PEW INTERNET & AMERICAN LIFE PROJECT, 35% OF AMERICAN ADULTS OWN A SMARTPHONE 9 (2011), *available at* http://www.pewinternet.org/~/media//Files/Reports/2011/PIP_Smartphones.pdf.

[7] Andrea McKenna, *Worlds of Difference in 'Mobile Money' Strategy*, AM. BANKER, Nov. 19, 2010, *available at* http://www.americanbanker.com/issues/175_223/mobile-money-strategy-from-haiti-1028902-1.html.

[8] Safaricom Ltd., M-PESA, http://www.safaricom.co.ke/index.php?id=250.

[9] *Id.* ("M-PESA Services").

[10] Google Wallet FAQ, http://www.google.com/wallet/faq.html#payments (last visited June 7, 2011).

[11] Elizabeth Woyke, *Bling Nation Prepares National Rollout of Mobile Payments, Handset Partnerships*, FORBES, Nov. 20, 2010, *available at* http://blogs.forbes.com/elizabethwoyke/2010/11/15/bling-nation-prepares-national-rollout-of-mobile-payments-handset-partnerships/; Dusan Belic, *Bling Nation Expands FanConnect to Austin*, INTOMOBILE, Mar. 29, 2011, *available at* http://www.intomobile.com/2011/03/29/bling-nation-expands-fanconnect-austin/.

[12] BD. OF GOVERNORS OF THE FED. RESERVE SYS., CONSUMERS AND MOBILE FINANCIAL SERVICES 1 (2012), *available at* http://www.federalreserve.gov/econresdata/mobile-device-report-201203.pdf.

[13] *See* Gail Hillebrand, *Before the Grand Rethinking: Five Things to do Today with Payments Law and Ten Prunciples to Guide New Payments and New Payments Law*, 83 CHI.-KENT L. REV. 769, 772-73 (2008) (discussing variation in protections among different payments methods).

[14] Prepaid card funds are typically held in pooled accounts. Regulation E's official staff interpretations appear to exempt funds in pooled accounts from the definition of "accounts" covered by the regulation. *See* Official Staff Interpretation of 12 C.F.R. § 205.2(b)(3), 12 C.F.R. § 205, Supplement I (2011).

[15] At present, these charges are typically for small-dollar text donations or digital content, but some companies are exploring the possibility of paying for other goods and services with prepaid phone deposits and phone bills. *See* Andrew Johnson, *Plan to Make the iPhone a Payment Tool May Accelerate*, AM. BANKER, Nov. 4, 2010, *available at* http://

www.americanbanker.com/issues/175_212/iphone-payment-tool-plan-1028195-1.html
(quoting Paul Grill, First Annapolis Consulting, who commented on "potential convergence
between the mobile and the e-commerce space," in which more types of goods are billed to
wireless plan).

[16] Consumers Union reviewed the customer contracts of the top wireless carriers, and found that
the protections carriers provide fall short of what consumers get when they use credit cards
and debit cards. In addition, many of the protections that wireless carrier representatives
maintain that they provide are not disclosed in customer contracts, making it difficult to
know whether consumers can count on these safeguards when problems arise. *See*
Consumers Union, How Top Wireless Companies Compare on Consumers Protections for
Mobile   Payments   (2011),   *available   at*   http://defendyourdollars.org/document/
how_top_wireless_carriers_compare_on_consumer_protections_for_mobile_payments.

[17] Section 1002 of the Dodd-Frank Wall Street Reform and Consumer Protection Act gives the
CFPB jurisdiction over "covered persons" providing consumer financial products or
services, including payments services. *See* Pub L. No. 111-203, 124 Stat. 1376, 1957-58
(2010).

[18] Title X of the Dodd-Frank Act transfers to the CFPB the authority to write rules under
consumer financial laws, including EFTA and TILA. *See* §§ 1002(12) and (14) and 1022(a),
124 Stat. at 1957, 1980.

INDEX

D

E

G

F

H